KINGFISHER
POCKET BOOK OF
MAGIC

Peter Eldin

Kingfisher Books

The author and the editor wish to thank
the following for their kind help in
the preparation of this book: Edwin A.
Dawes, Matt Limb, Samantha Salisbury,
James Townsend and Mac Wilson.

First published in 1985 by Kingfisher Books Limited
Elsley Court, 20-22 Great Titchfield Street,
London W1P 7AD
A Grisewood and Dempsey Company

Reprinted 1985

BRITISH LIBRARY CATALOGUING
IN PUBLICATION DATA
Eldin, Peter
  Pocket book of magic. – (Kingfisher pocket books)
  1. Conjuring – Juvenile literature
  I. Title
  793.8   GV1548
ISBN: 0 86272 121 0

Edited by Vanessa Clarke
Designed by Ben White
Illustrated by Jeane Colville, Jane Eccles/Fig 1,
Janos Marffy/Jillian Burgess, Annette Olney,
Mike Saunders/Jillian Burgess.
Cover design by Pinpoint Design Company
Phototypeset by Southern Positives and Negatives
(SPAN) Newchapel Road, Lingfield, Surrey.
Printed in Portugal.

Contents

The World of Magic

Welcome to the world of magic – a world where the laws of nature appear to be turned upside down and where the impossible is made to seem possible. Through the pages of this book you will learn some of the secrets of this fascinating art so that you, too, can become an expert magician.

Conjuring is one of the oldest forms of entertainment. It was first mentioned in writing in the *Westcar Papyrus* over 3500 years ago. This records how the great magician Jajamanekh recovered an ornament lost in a lake by splitting the lake in two and stacking one half on top of the other. After picking up the jewel, he returned to the shore, clapped his hands and the water fell back into place!

Since then there have been hundreds of records of magicians – working in the streets or at markets and fairs, or putting on shows in private houses and large theatres. Many are famous for creating specific tricks or elaborate illusions that still amaze and entertain audiences today. One of the greatest magicians of the past was the Frenchman Robert-Houdin whose 'Soirées Fantastiques' opened in Paris in 1845. He performed a wide range of magic and his presentation was completely original – he performed in ordinary evening dress rather than the long flowing robes of earlier magicians and treated magic in a scientific way. For this reason he is regarded as the 'father of modern magic'.

▶ **Marco** the Magi performing in a spectacular modern magic show.

◀ **The French magician,** Philippe, wore the robes of a wizard for his shows in the 1830s.

How To Start

The tricks described in this book have been carefully selected to give you an appreciation of some of the principles of magic. But simply knowing how a trick is done and how to carry it out will not make you a magician. The mechanics of an effect must be performed with skill but the *real* art of magic lies in the way that the trick is presented. As a magician you must be able to hide the method of the trick while convincing your audience that something absolutely extraordinary is taking place.

One technique you should try to develop is MISDIRECTION – the art of drawing the audience's attention away from secret moves. Use your hands and eyes to make them look where you want them to look. Camouflage what you are actually doing with a lively story or PATTER about the trick. Another equally important technique to develop is showmanship – the art of making people believe, by your movements, words or appearance, that you are truly a magician.

There are more details throughout this book on these techniques as well as suggestions on how to present tricks and feel your way to becoming a magician. The importance of practice is also emphasized. Do not show any trick until you have practised it thoroughly and never perform an EFFECT until you can do it so well that you do not have to worry about 'what comes next'. If you practise the tricks to perfection and think carefully about their presentation, you will be well on the way to becoming a good magician.

HOW TO USE THIS BOOK

Lots of tricks are explained in this book but do not try to learn them all at once. By all means read through the whole book if you wish. But then pick just one trick – that's right, just one – and learn it thoroughly. Examine it and see if you can improve it in any way. If you do not like a particular MOVE, try to think of another way of doing it. Think about your presentation – what you are going to say to your audience and how to misdirect them at crucial moments in your performance. How can you end the trick dramatically? Continue 'playing' with the trick in this way until you are happy with every aspect of it and you are confident that you can do it perfectly. Then move on to learn another trick. Not everyone's hands are the same, so if you find a particular move difficult or awkward see if you can adapt or change it to suit yourself.

▲ **Robert-Houdin** and his son with a mechanical orange tree which bore real fruit. Robert-Houdin was a watchmaker until he took up magic at the age of 40. He made several automata for his shows. His mind-reading routine with his son and an illusion in which his son rested horizontally in mid-air with only a single support under one arm created a sensation.

If you come across words in CAPITALS, look them up in the glossary on page 184 to find out exactly what they mean.

Whether or not you become a good magician is up to you. This book will give you a good start but you should also try to develop your knowledge and expertise by studying other books on conjuring (see page 182), by talking with other magicians (see page 181) and by further practice.

Equipment

All the tricks in this book can be performed with PROPS that are readily available. Many are every-day items you will find around the house, such as matches, envelopes, elastic bands and scissors. Where a trick uses a special piece of apparatus or a secret GIMMICK, instructions are given on how to make it. A few items, such as SILKS and rope, are best bought from a magic shop (see page 183), but to start with you can use ordinary hand-kerchiefs and ropes.

It is a good idea to build up a collection of the items illustrated opposite. Keep them in one place, for example in a magic box made from a cardboard carton and decorated with magic signs. In this way they will stay in good condition and will always be ready when you need them.

▲ **Magician's silks.** These coloured handkerchiefs are soft and fine which makes them easy to work with. When you start out you can use squares of chiffon or other lightweight material instead.

▲ **Do not buy** cheap playing cards for your tricks as they will soon become scruffy. But an old pack will be useful for practising.

◀ **Magician's rope** is very soft and particularly suited for magic.

Equipment

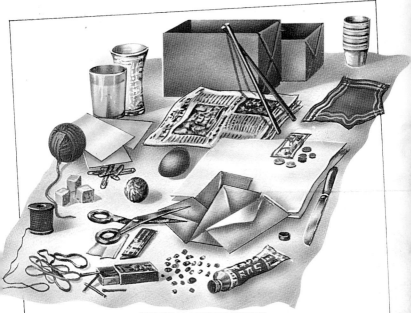

USEFUL EQUIPMENT

You will need these familiar objects to perform many of the tricks in this book; clockwise from the top they include:

Cardboard boxes
Paper cups
Handkerchief
Banknote
Coins
Paper
Envelopes
Table knife
Finger ring
Rubber cement
Beads
Matches
Rubber bands
Cigarette papers
Scissors
Thread
Sugar cubes
Ball
Paper clips
Egg
Ball of wool
Sheets of card
Glass tumblers
Newspaper
Wood dowelling

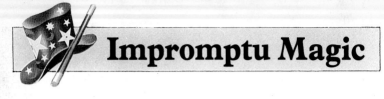

Impromptu Magic

As a magician you should be able to perform at a moment's notice with objects that are to hand wherever you may be. Alexander Herrmann, known in the late 1800s as 'Herrmann The Great', was famous for this kind of off-stage impromptu magic. When he travelled by taxi, the fare was always paid with money from the air, and when he ate out with friends their glasses disappeared and reappeared in the oddest places.

On the following pages are tricks that can be performed with little or no advance preparation. Some are very easy to do, but even so you should practise them carefully before showing them. With impromptu magic you must be ready to perform in places where the conditions are not ideal: places, for example, where it is too noisy for your spectators to hear the PATTER with which you build up a trick into a dramatic effect; or places where you are surrounded by people and have to be extremely careful not to let anyone spot your secret moves. The answer is to perfect several tricks and to present those that are most suitable for the setting. Always be aware of the position of your audience (see page 23) and stay adaptable – be prepared to swop to another trick to take advantage of any special circumstance or if something appears to go wrong.

▶ **Alexander Herrmann** was America's top magician from the 1870s until his death in 1896. His widow Adelaide, possibly the greatest lady magician of all time, joined with Alexander's nephew Leon for three years. Leon then toured with his own show, advertised by this poster, as 'Herrmann the Great'.

Jumping Elastic Band

Place an elastic band over the first two fingers of your left hand, near the base of the fingers (1). Hold your hand palm up.

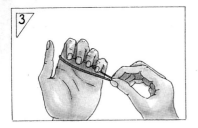

With the other hand begin to stretch the elastic band, emphasizing the fact that it is over the first two fingers only (2).

Begin to turn the left hand over and close it into a fist. As you do so, secretly slip the top of all four fingers into the elastic band (3). Immedi-

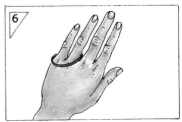

ately release the band from the right hand (4). It should look as if you have stretched the band and then let go as you turn your hand over.

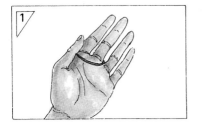

To the audience, which sees the back of the left hand, the band is still over the first two fingers. In fact all your fingers are inside (5).

Now open your hand and the elastic will appear to spring from the first two fingers to the other two by magic (6).

Initial Transfer

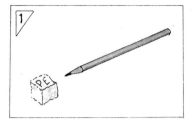

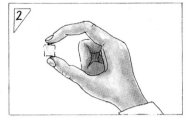

Equipment: One lump of sugar, a soft pencil, a glass of water.

Hand the sugar and the pencil to a spectator and ask her (or him) to write her initials in block capitals on one surface of the cube (1). While this is being done, secretly wet the ball of your thumb. One way to do this is to bring your hand up to your mouth as you pretend to cough.

Take the lump of sugar from the spectator and hold it so that the initials are against the ball of your damp thumb. Press the

cube firmly as you bring forward the glass of water (2). This transfers an impression of the spectator's initials onto your thumb. Drop the sugar into the water and ask the spectator to hold her hand over the glass.

To make sure the spectator's hand is in the correct position you guide it with your own hand. In doing this, you hold the spectator's hand with your thumb against her palm and your fingers on top of her hand. Press firmly and your thumb will 'print' the initials (3).

Ask her to watch the sugar dissolve and then to turn her hand over. Amazingly, there, on the palm, are her own initials (4).

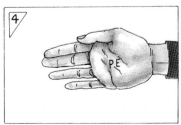

Chink a Chink

Equipment: Five sugar lumps, a table.

Place four sugar lumps on the table as in the picture below. Unknown to your audience, you have a fifth cube concealed in the right hand. The easiest way to hold this hidden piece is between the thumb and first finger at the base of the thumb. This is known to magicians as the THUMB PALM. Alternatively you can hold it in the palm of the hand as described on page 54.

Explain to your audience that you can only cover two cubes with your hands at any one time. Place your left hand on cube 1, your right hand on cube 4.

Change the position so that the hands now cover 3 and 4. As you move the right hand to cover 2, secretly pick up the cube at 3 and drop the concealed cube at 2. Raise your hands. There are now two cubes at 2 and none at 3. One cube has 'travelled' from one corner to the other.

Without pausing for too long, move your left hand (with its concealed cube) up to 2 as the right hand goes down to 4. Drop the concealed cube at 2 and pick up the cube at 4. Raise both hands to show that another invisible journey has been made.

Now cover 1 with the left hand and 2 with the right (concealing a cube). Lift up one cube at 1 and

drop the concealed cube at 2. Raise both hands and bring them both to the edge of the table to show all four cubes at 2.

Secretly drop the concealed cube on to your lap or into a pocket and the trick is over.

USING OTHER OBJECTS

Almost any small object can be used for this trick but cubes of sugar are the easiest because of their shape and rough surface. Try it with paper balls, dice or marbles. There are other routines for this trick but the one described here is the simplest and most straightforward. It is the basis for most of the alternative routines.

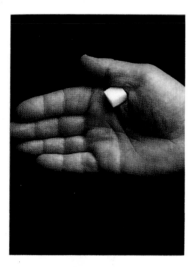

▲ **When holding** the sugar cube in the thumb palm position try to keep your hand relaxed. If it looks stiff it will be obvious to your audience that you are hiding something. Try to make all your actions as natural looking as you can. The only way to do this is to practise as much as you can. The great French magician Robert-Houdin used to walk around with his hands in his pockets so he could practise sleights at all times without anyone else knowing – an idea well worth copying.

Equipment: A silk scarf or a very large handkerchief.

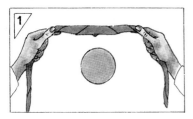

For this trick you will need the help of a member of your audience. Roll the scarf or handkerchief up into a long 'rope' and place it on top of the spectator's arm (1).

Take the ends below the arm and pretend to tie a knot (2). What you actually do is to take the centre of each side of the scarf, make two loops, and fold them together (3).

Pull the loops tight (4), then bring the two ends to the top, and tie as many knots as you can (5). It looks as if the scarf is now securely tied around the spectator's arm.

Take hold of the knotted ends, give a word of command, and pull upwards. The loops will come away from the arm giving the impression that it has gone straight through (6).

Journey Through a Postcard

Equipment: A postcard, scissors.

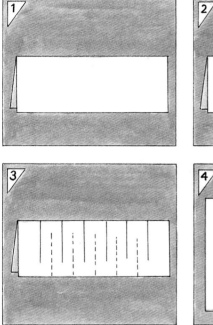

No one will believe you when you boast that you can make a hole in a postcard big enough to walk through.

To prove your claim you fold the postcard in half lengthways (1) and make cuts in it as shown by the dotted lines (2) and (3). The more cuts you make the easier the trick is to do. Unfold the card and make one straight cut from A to B (4). Carefully open out the card into a large circle and step through it.

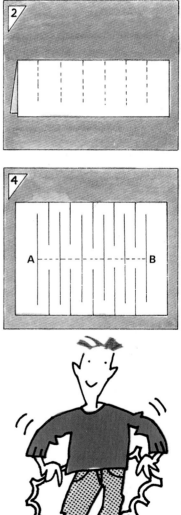

21

Squash

 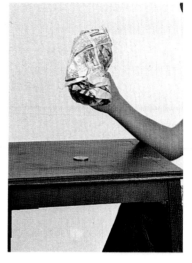

Equipment: A table, a chair, a coin, a glass tumbler, a sheet of newspaper.

This trick can be regarded as one of the classics of magic for it provides a good example of MISDIRECTION, the art of directing the audience's attention away from a secret move. Sit at the table and put the coin on top. Place the tumbler over it (1).

Announce that you are going to make the coin pass through the table but, as it must be done in secret, you cover the tumbler with a sheet of newspaper. Wrap the paper firmly around the glass so that its shape can be seen quite clearly (2).

Make some mystical passes over the tumbler. Pick up the glass through the newspaper but – much to your surprise – the coin is still there. Cover the coin with the paper-wrapped tumbler once more (2).

Make some more magical passes and then lift the tumbler again. This time bring the tumbler to the rear edge of the table as you lean forward in surprise – the coin is still there. While all attention is on the coin secretly allow the tumbler to drop from the paper on to your lap (3).

Say you will try once more and repeat the previous moves. Because the paper retains the shape of the tumbler no one will realize that in fact it is no longer there. After more mystical passes raise the 'tumbler' once again. The coin is still on the table. You now say, 'Maybe it would be easier to pass the glass through the table.' Then, crush the paper down on to the table top (4). The glass has vanished.

Reach under the table, remove the tumbler from your lap, and bring the tumbler into view as if it really had passed through the top of the table.

WATCH YOUR ANGLES

A magician should be aware of the position of the spectators at all times. In Squash it is essential that the audience is in front of the magician. Anyone at the sides could see the tumbler when it falls on to the lap. This can be screened by leaning forward at the crucial moment but such action must be natural if it is to succeed. In a number of tricks, particularly with SLEIGHT-OF-HAND, the angles at which the spectators look at you can be vital and you must be aware of these when practising. This is why it is often useful to practise in front of a mirror (see page 166).

If there is any chance of a spectator seeing your secret moves there are three things you can do:

1. Ask the spectator, or spectators, to move 'so that they will get a better view'.
2. Move yourself until you are satisfied with the position.
3. Do a different trick from the one you had planned.

Topsy Turvy Note

It is often said that 'the quickness of the hand deceives the eye'. This is simply not true, for the eye is so sensitive that it will easily catch any quick movement made by the magician. Some tricks, in fact, are more spectacular because they are performed slowly. This is one of them.

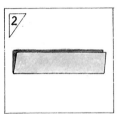

Hold a banknote the right way up and facing the audience (1). The illustrations show each move from the audience's point of view. Fold the note up from the bottom to fold it in half lengthways (2). Fold it in half towards you (3).

Fold it in half again (4). Pause for a second. Hold the note steady in clear view of the audience. Look at the note as if something is puzzling you about it. Now unfold it from the front (5), (6). Continue to make your movements as slow, deliberate, and as mysterious as you can.

When, at last, the note is completely unfolded it is seen to have miraculously turned itself upside down (7). Although the slow-motion working sequence is automatic this trick is extremely effective if presented correctly.

Anti-Magnetic Matches

Place a used match on your left hand with its head overhanging your palm. Hold a second used match halfway along its length between the thumb and first finger of the right hand. The edge of the nail of the second finger of this hand is positioned against the end of the match, on the same side as the first finger (1).

Bring the right hand, palm downwards, towards the left until the two match heads almost touch. Just before they make contact flick the end of the right-hand match with your fingernail. The impact will cause the head of this match to strike the other with such force that the left-hand match will leap from your hand and into the air (2).

As the attention of the spectators is focused on the spectacularly dramatic movement of the match springing from your left hand no one notices the small flick made by the match in the right hand.

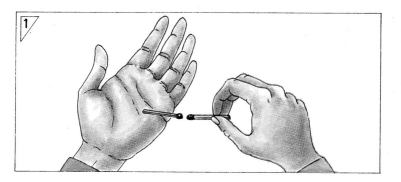

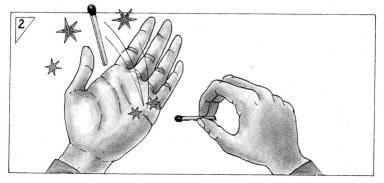

One in the Pocket

The theme of this trick appears in many conjuring tricks. It is rather like Cups and Balls (see page 118) – but without the cups.

Equipment: A sheet of newspaper.
Preparation: Take a piece of newspaper, about 10 cm (4 in) square, and roll it into a ball. Take a much smaller piece of newspaper and roll it into a small pellet. Place the pellet in your right jacket pocket and the large ball in the same pocket.
Performance: When someone asks to see a trick casually place your right hand into your jacket pocket and STEAL the pellet as you request the use of a newspaper. Keep the pellet

secretly concealed, clipped between the first and second fingers, as you form three similar pellets from the newspaper. When you have made them place these three pellets on the table (1).

Pick up one pellet with the right hand and drop it into your left as you count, 'One'. Do the same with the second pellet, 'Two'. But this time you also drop the hidden pellet into the left hand. Pretend to put the third pellet from the table into your right pocket, actually retaining it in your right hand, as you say: 'And one in the pocket.'

Pause for a second or two. Open the left hand and allow the three pellets to drop on to the table (2).

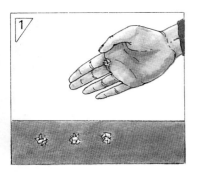

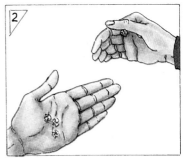

USING OTHER OBJECTS

This trick is a useful one to know as it can be performed any-where, with very little advance preparation, and with most small objects. For example try:
1. Three plum stones and a final whole plum.
2. Three broken matches and a complete match.

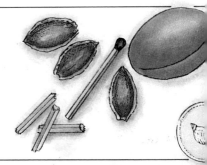

Pick up two of the pellets in your right fingers and drop them, together with the concealed pellet, into your left hand. Again you say, 'Two in the hand and one in the pocket,' as you pick up the third pellet and place it into the right pocket. This time you really do drop it into the pocket but you also secretly remove the large ball of paper. As your right hand comes out of the pocket the audience's attention is concentrated on the left hand which has opened to reveal that it contains not two, but three pellets once again (3).

Now pick up two of the pellets from the table and pretend to drop them into your left hand as before, as you say, 'Two in the hand.' In actual fact, you drop the concealed large ball of paper and retain the two pellets in your right hand. As you say 'And one in the pocket' you pick up the third pellet with your right hand and drop all three pellets into your pocket. Look at the audience as you do this. They, in turn, will be more likely to look at your face and will not notice that you have more than one pellet in your right hand.

Ask how many pellets there are now in the left hand. Some will say two, others, having been caught twice already, will say three. But you prove them all wrong when you open your hand for you have only one – one that is much larger than the others you have been using (4).

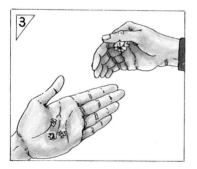

3. Three coins and a larger coin or a folded banknote.
4. Three pebbles and a large stone.
  The list is endless and limited only by your ingenuity and the size of your pockets. See if you can think up some other objects that you can use for this trick.

Han Ping Chien Coins

Equipment: Six coins of the same size, one finger ring or smaller coin. This trick is performed sitting at a table.

Lay the six coins down in two rows of three as illustrated below. Pick up the ring in the right hand and the three coins from the right column in the same hand. Secretly position these coins so they are held in the crotch of the thumb, between thumb and forefinger – see right.

Pick up the other three coins in the left hand and say: 'Three coins in the left hand' and slap them down on to the table.

Pick up the coins again but hold them so that they are at the bottom of the fist (alongside the left little finger).

Place the left fist on the table top about 10 cm (4 in) from your right hand. Say: 'And three coins and a ring in my right hand' as you apparently drop the coins and ring on to the table. What you actually do is release only the ring from the right hand.

At the same moment you move the left fist to the left, leaving its three coins on the table as the right hand comes down on top of them. When the right hand is raised three coins and a ring can be seen. They appear to have come from the right hand but this hand, unknown to the audience, still holds

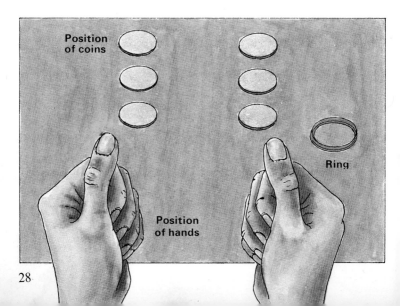

Position of coins

Ring

Position of hands

its original three coins. It is upon this move that the whole trick depends. The move in itself is not difficult but it does require practice.

Pick up the three coins and the ring with the right hand. The pick-up must appear to be natural and yet you must also be very careful not to drop any of the hidden coins or to give any indication of their presence. Place the right hand underneath the table.

Slap your left hand on to the table top and then lift the hand to show that the coins have gone. Remove the right hand from beneath the table and roll all six coins and the ring on to the table top. It appears that the three coins in the left hand have passed through the top of the table.

Now lay out the coins in two rows once again and offer to repeat the trick.

Pick up the ring and the three right-hand coins in the right hand and then place that hand under the table as you pick up the coins from the left column. Say: 'Three coins in this hand,' as you slap the coins from the left hand on to the table. At the same time you secretly deposit the three coins from your right hand on to your lap or right knee. The left hand picks up the three coins as

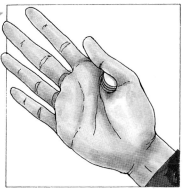

▲ The thumb palm.

the right hand is removed from beneath the table. Once again the coins are held at the bottom of the left fist and the hand is left lying on the table top.

Bring the right hand (which contains only the ring) down to the table and perform the same movement as before (releasing the three coins from the left hand) so it looks as if three coins and a ring have come from the right hand. Say: 'And three coins and a ring in this hand.'

Allow your audience to see that your right hand is empty as you pick up the coins and the ring in your right hand. Place your right hand beneath the table. Slap your left hand down on the table – the coins have gone. Bring the right hand from beneath the table, gathering the coins from your leg as you do so, and open it to reveal all six coins and the ring. It appears that the coins have penetrated the table top yet again.

29

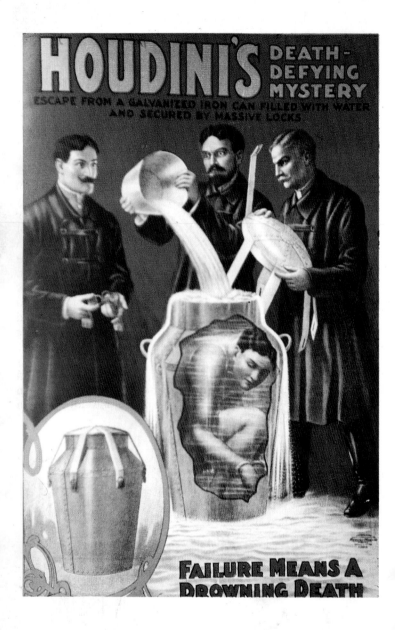

Stage Magic

As the title of this chapter suggests, the tricks in this section are designed to be performed on a stage. But you do not have to be on a stage to perform them as long as you are at least two metres (six feet) from your audience. Certain tricks are more suited to stage magic than to CLOSE-UP magic. The PROPS used may be too large or cumbersome for close-up work, for example, or it may be that the secret would be revealed if the magician is too close to the audience.

Two illusions are included in this section. To a magician an illusion is a big spectacular trick usually involving people or animals. Many magicians are famous for particular illusions they have created. In the 1830s, John Henry Anderson, 'The Wizard of the North', was one of the first magicians to pull a rabbit from a hat. Robert-Houdin perfected huge numbers of illusions, in one of which he suspended his young son in space. Vanishing acts are particularly spectacular: Houdini caused an elephant to disappear, Kalanag vanished a motor car while the American magician, David Copperfield once made a full-size aircraft disappear. Other illusionists, such as Ziegfried and Roy, baffle audiences by splitting girls into three parts or making them float in the air.

In most cases illusions require expensive equipment which puts them beyond the means of most amateur and many professional magicians. The ones in this section, however, – Production Extraordinaire and the Incredible Sword Box – will not cost you much to make and still amaze your audience.

◀ **In 1908 Harry Houdini** introduced the Milk Can escape into his act. He stepped into an iron canister filled with water. The lid was secured with six padlocks. Within a few minutes Houdini was on the outside and the canister was still locked.

Houdini Silk

In this trick, a SILK, representing the great escapologist Harry Houdini, 'escapes' from a sealed glass tumbler – just like Houdini escaping from a police cell.

Equipment: Two silks of different colours, a larger silk scarf, 20–25 cm (8–10 in) of cotton thread, a glass tumbler, an elastic band.

Preparation: Tie the length of cotton to one corner of the silk that is to represent Houdini.

Performance: In performance you PATTER about Houdini as you put the Houdini silk into the tumbler. In doing this, make sure the thread is hanging outside the glass (1). Put the second silk in the tumbler on top of the first. Now throw the scarf over the mouth of the tumbler and hold it in place with the elastic band (2).

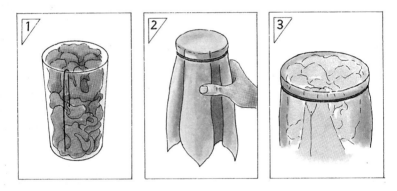

Tell your audience that it is now impossible for 'Houdini' to escape from his sealed prison. Reach beneath the scarf and take hold of the thread (to help you do this it is a good idea to have a knot at the end of the thread). Pull the thread and the Houdini silk will be pulled out of the glass (3). Make sure you use an elastic band that is loose enough to enable you to do this. Grasp the corner of the silk and pull it into view as if it is being pulled through the bottom of the glass (4).

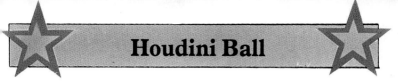

In this trick a small ball is used to represent Houdini. Although imprisoned in a securely tied bag, Houdini manages to escape.

Equipment: Two identical cloth bags, a small ball, a length of rope or ribbon, a large scarf.

Performance: Place one bag inside the other and hold the two so that the neck of the inner bag is concealed by your hand (1).

Ask a spectator to drop the ball (Houdini) into the bag; it will fall into the outer bag. Now draw the spectator's attention to the length of rope or ribbon lying on the table. As the rope is being fetched, change your grip on the bags so that it looks as if you are grasping the neck of the bag. In fact your fingers are concealing the top of the outer bag; and the material seen above your hand is actually the inner bag, but to the audience they seem to be one complete bag.

Ask the spectator to tie the neck of the bag with the rope. It will actually be the neck of the inner bag that is tied.

Get one spectator to hold one end of the rope and another spectator to hold the opposite end. Throw a scarf over the bags. Place both your hands beneath the scarf, pull off the outer bag and remove the ball.

Bring the ball into view and casually throw the scarf (with the outer bag hidden within its folds) on to the table. The audience can see that the bag is still tied on the rope and yet Houdini has escaped. The bag, rope and ball can be examined by the spectators but there seems to be no logical explanation as to how this miracle was accomplished.

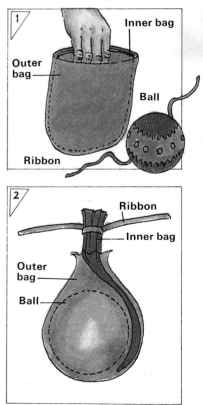

33

Going Up

Tube

Cubes

Equipment: Four red cubes, one green cube, a cardboard tube, open at each end (just wide enough to take the cubes) and tall enough to hold all five cubes.

Preparation: Put one of the red cubes into the tube. Hold it so that pressure from your fingers keeps the red cube at the bottom of the tube and stops it falling out and being seen.

Performance: Put the tube on the table. Pick up the green cube and drop it into the tube. Drop the other three (red) cubes in on top. Now lift the tube holding it at the top and gripping tightly enough to retain the topmost cube. When the pile of cubes is revealed the green cube is not at the bottom of the pile as everyone expects but appears to have jumped up one place.

Turn the tube upside down and put it back on the table so that the hidden red cube is at the bottom. Put in one red cube, then the green cube, and then the rest of the cubes. The green cube should now be second from the bottom of the pile but when you lift the tube again it has jumped into third place. Keep one cube in the tube at the top as before by tightening your grip.

Repeat the actions, so that this time the green cube jumps to the top of the pile. Knock the pile of cubes over and place the tube down behind them, making sure that your audience doesn't see the extra red cube.

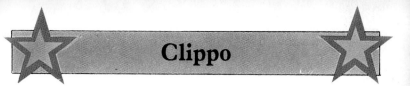
Equipment: A sheet of newspaper, rubber cement, talcum powder, sharp scissors.

Preparation: From the double page of a large-format newspaper cut a strip about 5 cm (2 in) wide. Fold the strip in half along what was the centre crease of the newspaper. Open out the strip and apply a wide area of rubber cement to the inside(1). Spread out evenly and allow it to dry. Repeat this twice allowing the cement to dry between applications. Now sprinkle talcum powder over the glued area.

Performance: Show the strip and fold it in half. Cut through both halves about 2 cm ($\frac{3}{4}$ in) beneath the fold (2). Logically you should have two separate strips of paper. But, if you take the end of one and let the other fall you appear to have only one (3). A thin film of rubber cement (pressed together when you cut through the paper) holds the two together. This trick can be repeated several times – depending on how far you applied the rubber cement.

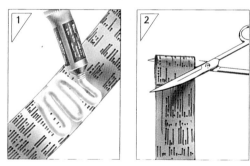

A CONTINUITY GAG

Clippo, although a good trick, needs some thought regarding its presentation if it is to be more than a mere puzzle. One way is to use it as a CONTINUITY GAG – a joke that is repeated several times during a performance. After every trick you perform you could pick up the strip and say: 'For my next trick I need two strips of paper.' You cut the strip apparently in two, but it remains in one piece. Shrug your shoulders, put the strip down, and do your next trick. Repeated several times during your act, this should bring a smile of amusement to the faces of your spectators.

Newton Outdone

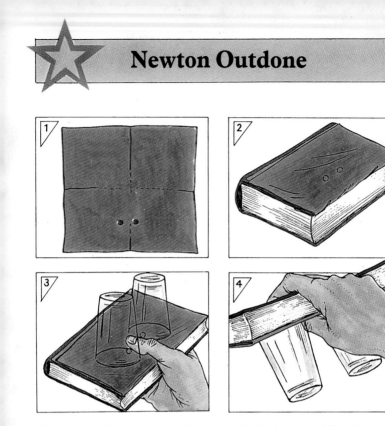

Equipment: Two glass tumblers, one book, one handkerchief, two small beads the same colour as the handkerchief.

Preparation: Sew the two beads on to the handkerchief about a quarter of the way from one edge. The distance between the two beads should be fractionally more than the width of your thumb – see picture (1).

This trick would have baffled Sir Isaac Newton for it appears to contradict the laws of gravity. Place the handkerchief on a table

with the book and the glasses and you are ready to perform.

Show the handkerchief to the audience. Keep the side on which the beads are sewn towards you so they cannot be seen. Fold the handkerchief in half with the beads on the inside.

Lay the handkerchief on the book. Open the book slightly and tuck the ends of the handkerchief into it to stop them hanging down at a later stage (2).

Now hold the book, with the handkerchief on top, in one hand. Your fingers should be underneath the book, the thumb on top. The positioning of the thumb is important. It *must* be between the two beads (3).

Pick up one of the tumblers and place it upside down on top of the handkerchief. One of the beads should go just inside the rim of the tumbler. In other words, part of the rim of the tumbler should be in between one bead and your thumb. Look at illustration (3) and you will see exactly what this looks like. Now place the second tumbler, also upside down, on the other side of your thumb. Both tumblers are now trapped between your thumb and the beads. In fact they are held so securely (if you have positioned the beads correctly) that you can turn your hand over. To the amazement of your audience the tumblers do not fall to the ground but remain under the book, defying the laws of gravity (4).

Wave your free hand over and under the book and the tumblers so that everyone can see that nothing but magic is holding the tumblers in place. As the audience applauds, turn the book over and remove the tumblers. Pull off the handkerchief and place it in your pocket. Then flick through the pages of the book as if trying to find out how the trick was done and take your bow.

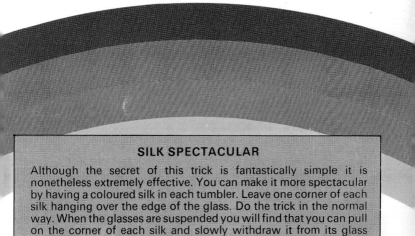

SILK SPECTACULAR

Although the secret of this trick is fantastically simple it is nonetheless extremely effective. You can make it more spectacular by having a coloured silk in each tumbler. Leave one corner of each silk hanging over the edge of the glass. Do the trick in the normal way. When the glasses are suspended you will find that you can pull on the corner of each silk and slowly withdraw it from its glass without either of the glasses falling. It looks absolutely amazing!

The Sterling Egg

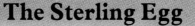

The Sterling Egg, named after Max Sterling, is a truly magical effect but one that requires a lot of preparation. It is, however, worth the effort.

Equipment: Two eggs (one white hen's egg and one duck's egg – if you can't buy a duck's egg a hen's egg will do), a pin, vinegar, a jar, a small tin, talcum powder, a sheet of white tissue paper, a glass tumbler, a fan, two hooks, a table.

Preparation: With a pin, make a hole in both ends of the duck's egg and blow out the white and the yolk into a bowl. Very carefully, for it is extremely fragile, wash out the inside of the egg under clean running water. Now put it in a jar of vinegar and leave it there for a week. The vinegar will dissolve the shell, leaving the thin membrane inside. Wash this fine egg-skin and allow it to dry. When not in use, keep it in a small tin full of talcum powder to preserve it.

Fix the two hooks to the rear edge of your table (the edge nearest to you) to hold the real

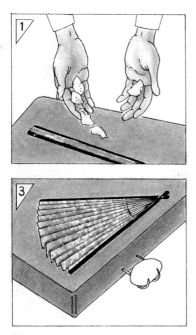

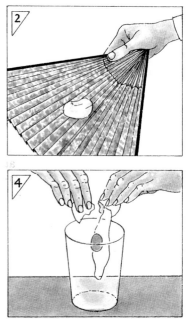

38

egg until it is required. Put the fan on top of the table – you can use a book or a piece of card instead if you wish.

Performance: Show the sheet of tissue paper, behind which you hold the egg-skin. Tear the paper into small pieces and pretend to take one (but, in fact, take the egg-skin) in your left hand (1). Drop the other pieces on to the table, pick up the fan, and place the skin on it.

Now bounce the skin up and down on the fan (2). Do this with a slight sideways movement so that the skin is revolving when it is in the air. Gradually the skin will fill with air and take on the shape of an egg. Stop fanning and allow the skin to roll on to your left hand. Keep the hand flat so that the 'egg' can be seen.

Replace the fan on your table, near the rear edge, at the same time STEALING the real egg from the hooks (3). Do *not* look down when you do this. If you look at the table at this point the audience will do the same and see you pick up the real egg. Keep your eyes on the inflated egg-skin on your left hand. Bring the right hand, concealing the real egg, up and over the skin. And, with the real egg, squash the skin flat, at the same time allowing the real egg to be seen.

▲ **Performing** The Sterling Egg. If you have a particularly interesting fan, try inventing a story around it when you perform this baffling trick.

Keeping the egg-skin concealed, break the egg into the tumbler (4), and drop the broken shell, together with the concealed skin, into a waste-paper basket. Make sure that you can recover the skin after the show or you will have to make another one.

Pick up the glass, hold it up at the level of your face for a few seconds for the audience to appreciate what you have just accomplished, and then bow to acknowledge their applause.

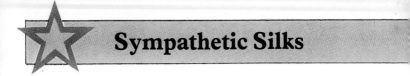

Sympathetic Silks

Six large SILKS are shown. Three are placed on a chair and the remaining three are tied together and placed on the table. When the silks are lifted from the chair they are seen to have tied themselves together in sympathy with those on the table.

The knots connecting the three 'chair' silks are undone. When the three silks are lifted from the table they are seen to have undone themselves also. As a finale you throw all six silks into the air where they tie themselves together.

Equipment: A small elastic band (your skin colour), six large silks (each about 70 cm/28 in square), a chair and a table.

Preparation: Prepare for the trick by placing the elastic band over the little finger of the left hand and tying three of the silks together as shown (1). Drape the three tied silks over the back of the chair. Drape the three loose silks over the back of the same chair but position them to one side of the first three silks (2).

Performance: Pick up one of the loose silks and place its top corner in between the thumb and first finger of the left hand. Now pick up the top corners of the three tied silks one by one. Place these corners in between the first and second fingers of the left hand. The two

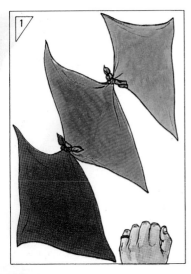

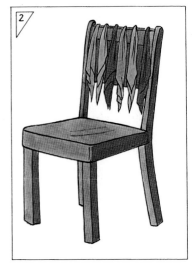

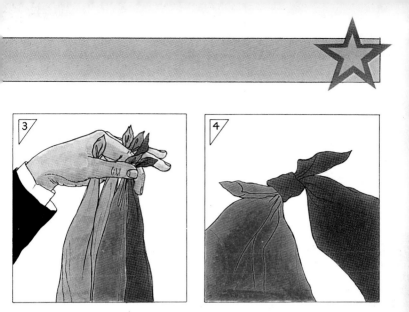

remaining silks are then picked up and their top corners are placed between the first finger and thumb of the left hand but as far away as possible from the first silk (3).

All of these movements should be practised thoroughly. From the audience's point of view it should seem that you have simply picked up the silks from the back of the chair and placed them into your left hand.

Now, for the first time, you draw attention to the silks and apparently count them from one hand to the other. In order to convince the spectators that all six silks are separate you must employ a FALSE COUNT. The smooth execution of this false count is essential to the success of the trick so practise it thoroughly before performing it in public.

With both hands held out in front of you, take the first silk in your right hand as you count 'One'. Bring the right hand back to the left and remove the second loose silk as you count 'Two'. Once again bring both hands together for the removal of the third silk. What you actually do at this point is replace one and two between the first finger and thumb of the left hand. At the same time the first and second fingers of the right hand remove the three tied silks from the first and second fingers of the left hand as you count 'Three'.

Properly done, the illusion of counting three separate silks is absolutely perfect. You should now have the three tied silks in your right hand and the three single silks in your left hand. Without pausing continue to count the three single silks from your left hand one at a time as you count, 'Four, Five, Six'. Take the three tied silks and, still handling them as if separate, drop them on to a chair.

Place the three single silks over your crooked left arm. Remove two of them and tie them together at one corner. Use a reef knot to tie the two silks together but do not tighten it too much (4). You now appear to tighten the knot but what you really do is take hold of one of the silks on each side of the knot and pull sharply. This straightens the silk you are pulling and converts the knot into a slip knot. You will now find that you can easily slide the second silk off the first – but in performance you do not do this straight away.

Now take the diagonally opposite corner of the first silk and tie it to one corner of the third. Pull the first silk as if tightening the knot and once again the knot is converted into a slip knot so that the third silk can be slipped off the first when required. Display the three knotted silks between both hands. In doing this hold the knots between the thumb and forefinger of each hand (5).

The next move should look as if you simply bundle the silks together and drop them on to your table. What you actually do is grasp the centre (first) silk below the knots with the little finger of each

hand. You will now find that you can use the first finger and thumb of each hand to push the knots off each end of the centre (first) silk. As soon as this is done drop all three silks into one pile on your table.

The audience believes that these three silks are still tied together but you have secretly separated them right before their eyes. You now draw attention to the silks on the chair. (The audience believes these to be separate.) Lift them up to show they are all tied together.

Untie the knots to separate the silks. While you are untying them remove the elastic band from your finger and place it over all the fingers and thumb of the left hand. As soon as each silk is released tuck one corner of it into the elastic band (6).

Now draw attention to the silks on the table. The audience believes these to be tied together. They will be very surprised when you lift each silk separately – completely detached from each other. As each silk is shown separately it is casually placed on the left hand (and into the elastic band).

As a final flourish you throw all the silks into the air and catch them. They now seem to be tied together but in fact they are held together by the elastic band. Take your bow, place the silks on the table, and then go on to your next trick.

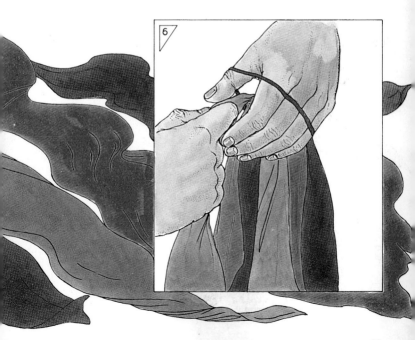

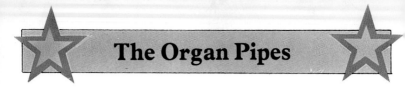

The Organ Pipes

Equipment: Two sheets of cartridge paper each about 20 cm (8 in) by 30 cm (12 in), five paper clips, about 12 cm (5 in) of dark thread, two elastic bands, ribbons and silks.

Preparation: Form each piece of paper into a tube, holding it in position by a paper clip at the top and the bottom (1). One of the tubes must be a little thinner than the other. Now roll up all the silks and the ribbons into one ball and put the elastic bands around them to hold them in place. Bend a paper clip into an S-shaped hook and tie one end of the thread to it. The other end of the thread is attached to one of the elastic bands. Put the ball of ribbons into the thinner of the two tubes and place the hook over the top edge of the tube so that when the tube is picked up the silks and ribbons hang inside, out of sight.

Performance: To perform this trick you first show the wider tube empty. Then casually drop the smaller tube through it and out the other end (2). During this movement the hook catches on the rim of the wide tube and the silks and ribbons are transferred from one tube to the other (3) and (4). Now show that the smaller tube is empty. Having shown both tubes empty place the wide tube over the narrow tube and place both tubes together on your left hand or on a table (5). Put your right hand into the top of the two tubes, remove the elastic bands, and pull out the ribbons and silks (6).

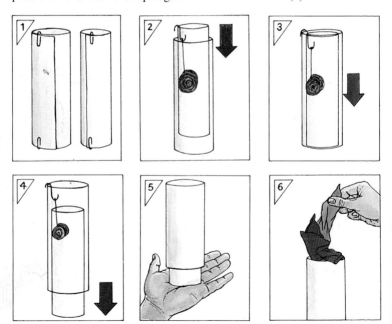

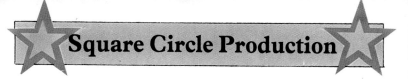

Square Circle Production

An important principle of magic is that anything painted black will not be visible when placed against a black background. The square circle production makes use of this principle.

Equipment: Two open-ended cubes of wood or cardboard (one slightly smaller than the other), a small 'production' box (open at top) to fit within the inner cube, silks and ribbons.

Preparation: The small box and the insides of the two cubes must be painted matt black. The outsides of the two cubes should be painted in bright colours. At the front of the larger cube cut out a window as shown in the illustration (1). Fill the black box with a quantity of silks and ribbons. Place the inner cube over the box and the outer cube over both and you are ready (2).

Performance: Pick up the outer cube, show the audience that it is empty and place it back in position (3). Take out the inner cube and show this to be empty also (4). At this stage the audience believes that they can see through to the interior of the outer cube because of the cut-out window. But as the interior of the cube is black and the 'production box' is also black they do not realize that there is something concealed inside.

Place the inner cube back into position, wave your hand over the boxes, and then produce the silks and ribbons (5).

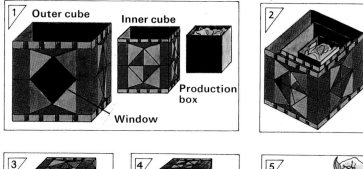

Outer cube · Inner cube · Production box · Window

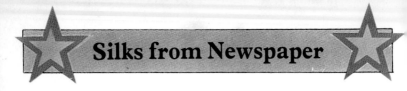

Equipment: A sheet of news-paper, silks, a small box, adhesive tape, a thin strip of metal.

Preparation: You will need to make a secret piece of apparatus out of a small box to do this trick. Find a small box or carton about the size of a matchbox open at one end. With some strong adhesive tape, attach a thin metal

Use the metal 'clip' to hold the box at the back of your right hand. To do this, put the ends of the clip on either side of the middle finger.

Performance: Stand with your left side towards the audience. Hold the newspaper in your right hand with the box hidden from the audience (3).

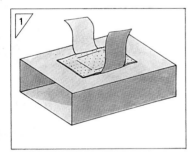

strip to the back of the box (1). Paint both the box and the metal strip the colour of your skin to disguise them.

Push a silk into the box but leave one corner sticking up-wards. Take a second silk, wrap one corner of it around the corner of the first silk (2) and then push both into the box (again leaving one corner of the second silk sticking up). Do the same with the remaining silks until the box is full. The way that the silks are looped together will make it easier to remove them during the trick.

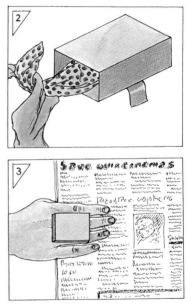

Take the bottom of the news-paper with your left hand. Let go of the top of the newspaper and bring the bottom up to the right hand (4). This move shows both sides of the newspaper. It also reveals the right hand which

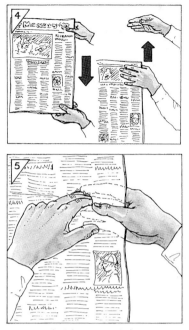

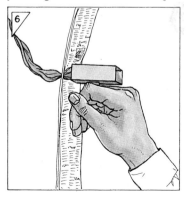

must be held out straight to keep the box hidden.

Move your right hand nearer to the centre of the newspaper at the nearest edge. Punch a hole in the paper at that point with the fingers of the left hand. Bend your right hand so that the open

end of the box is against the back of the newspaper. The left fingers now reach into the hole just formed (and into the box) and pull out about half the length of the first silk (5) and (6).

Move the right hand back and then up to its former position at the top of the sheet. This pulls the remaining half of the silk from the box. Because of the way the silks are looped together this movement also brings one corner of the next silk close to the opening of the box ready for the next production.

Leave the silk hanging from the newspaper. Repeat the 'turn-over' move (4) to show there is nothing hidden behind the newspaper and then produce a silk from somewhere else on the page, repeating steps (5) and (6).

When all the silks have been produced, remove them all from the paper. Secretly bend the right hand so that the box comes into contact with the rear of the newspaper (7). Casually screw the newspaper up into a loose ball – wrapping it around the box in the process so that your hands are completely empty.

Production Extraordinaire

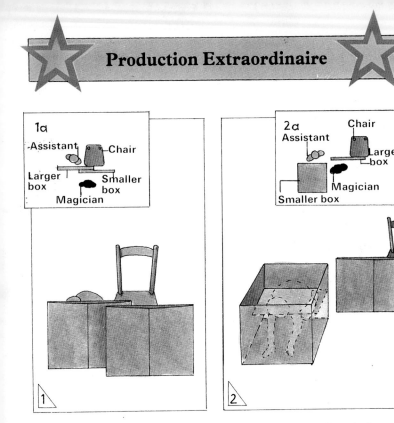

1a
-Assistant
Chair
Larger box
Smaller box
Magician

2a
Chair
Assistant
Larger box
Magician
Smaller box

1

2

If a trick employs large apparatus or involves the vanishing, production or apparent mutilation of people, magicians refer to it as an ILLUSION. Most illusions require expensive apparatus but here is one that will cost absolutely nothing.

Equipment: Two cardboard boxes or cartons, each one big enough to conceal a person. One box must be slightly larger than the other – try your local supermarket for these. A chair.

Preparation: Cut off both the top and the bottom of the two boxes or cartons to turn them into tubes rather than boxes. Then cut a large flap like a door in the smaller of the two cartons. It must be big enough for your assistant to crawl through. Fold both cartons flat and lean them against a chair. Put the smaller 'prepared' carton in front with the flap to the rear. The person you are going to produce hides behind the rear carton (1) and (1a). Make sure that he or she cannot be seen by the audience.

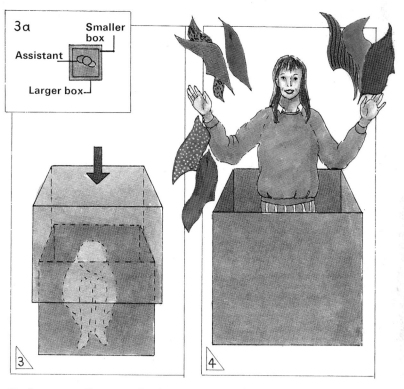

Performance: Remove the front carton and show that it is completely flat. Be careful that you don't allow the audience to see the flap when you do this.

Open out the carton and place it on the stage. You must position yourself so that your body conceals the space between the open carton and the flat carton still leaning on the chair (2a). Keep your legs closed for it is at this point that your assistant creeps from behind the flat carton to the rear of the opened carton (2). Your assistant now crawls through the flap and into the opened carton.

You now pick up the second carton and open it out to show it is empty. Place this carton over the one standing on the stage (3) and (3a). You can now turn the two cartons around to show all sides as the outer carton conceals the flap in the inner carton.

When you clap your hands your assistant jumps up into view (4) and you both take a bow. If you have a *very* well trained dog perhaps you can persuade it to be your assistant!

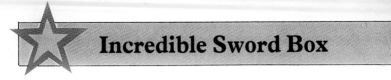

Incredible Sword Box

Equipment: A cardboard box or carton just large enough for your assistant to sit in, ten pieces of wooden dowelling long enough to pass right through the box.

The ILLUSION in which the magician thrusts swords through a box containing an assistant is very popular. This version of the classic illusion can be set up relatively cheaply.

First of all you need to make holes in the sides of the carton to allow the wooden dowelling 'swords' to pass through it. To get these holes in the correct places, your assistant must sit in the box and guide the 'swords' to the exact spot. The big secret of this illusion is that your assistant does not sit in the box the way the audience thinks he is sitting. You show the box to your audience and your assistant steps into the box facing the audience. He (or she) then sits down inside but, as soon as he is out of sight, he turns sideways on – see the illustration on the opposite page.

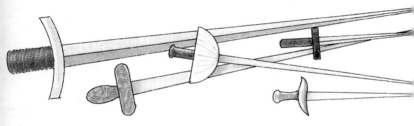

You then push the first 'sword' through the centre of the box from front to rear. If your assistant was sitting facing the audience, as the spectators believe, it would go right through the centre of his body, but as he is sitting sideways it simply passes harmlessly in front of him. All the remaining 'swords' are pushed through the box and apparently through your unfortunate assistant. It seems impossible that he can remain unharmed.

You now remove all the 'swords' one by one. Your assistant inside the box turns to face the front once again and then stands up – to thunderous applause from the spectators!

It is a good idea to paint designs on the wooden 'swords' and to cover the carton with coloured paper. For added effect stick on stars and other conjuring symbols.

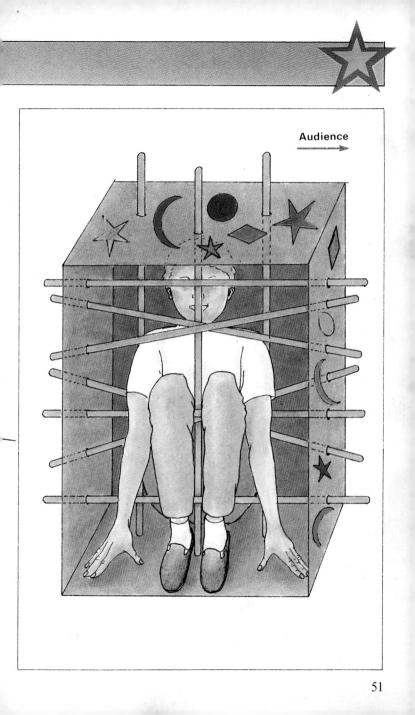

Audience

Magic Money

Most people enjoy magic and most people are interested in money. It is, therefore, not surprising that magic with money is particularly appealing to audiences all over the world. Coin tricks are also very old. In *The Discoverie of Witchcraft* (1584), Reginald Scot describes several effects with coins that bamboozled and amused spectators as much then as they do to this day.

One trick with money that is particularly fascinating to audiences is The Miser's Dream in which the magician plucks coins from thin air. Although performed before his time in one form or another this effect is particularly associated with T. Nelson Downs (born 1867) who specialized in magic with coins. One of the most spectacular versions of this effect was Chung Ling Soo's Dream of Wealth in which showers of silver coins poured from a metal box, banknotes were produced in their hundreds, and an enormous banknote filled the stage. Suddenly the large note disappeared and a large gold coin was seen hanging in the centre of the stage. Sections of the coin moved to reveal a girl carrying a cornucopia from which streamed a seemingly endless shower of gold coins.

You can use any coins for the coin effects in this chapter but you will find that coins with milled edges are easier to manipulate than those with plain rims. Coin tricks that can be shown anytime and anywhere are especially useful and you will find tricks like the Classic Palm Vanish, Coin Escape, Travelling Coin and Through the Hand are well worth learning.

◀ **T. Nelson Downs**
(1867–1938) was a magician who specialized in magic with coins. The poster, shown here, displays the variety of his coin manipulations – an act that has never been equalled.

Classic Palm Vanish

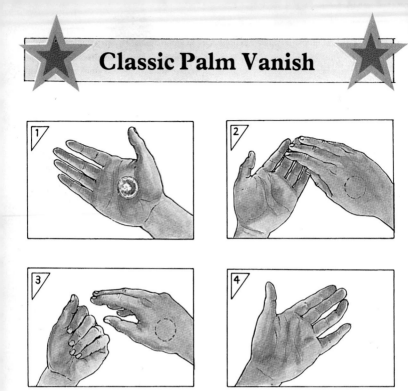

Show a coin on the palm of your right hand at the base of your thumb (1). Hold the left hand palm up and transfer the coin by turning the open right hand over the left. Withdraw the empty right hand and close the left covering the coin. Do this several times in front of the mirror to see the exact movements that you make each time.

Now do the same again but just before turning the right hand over tighten the muscles at the base of the right thumb and the fourth finger to retain the coin in the right hand (2). This is known as PALMING. Close the left hand

as if containing the coin and allow the right hand to fall to the side (3).

Try to forget the fact that you have the coin in your right hand. Convince yourself that the coin is in the left hand and you will have a better chance of convincing the audience. This is a basic rule of MISDIRECTION – look where you want the audience to look. After a few seconds open the left hand, finger by finger, to show that the coin has vanished (4).

Performed well this is an extremely convincing vanish. Practise it until all your movements are completely natural.

Coin Fold

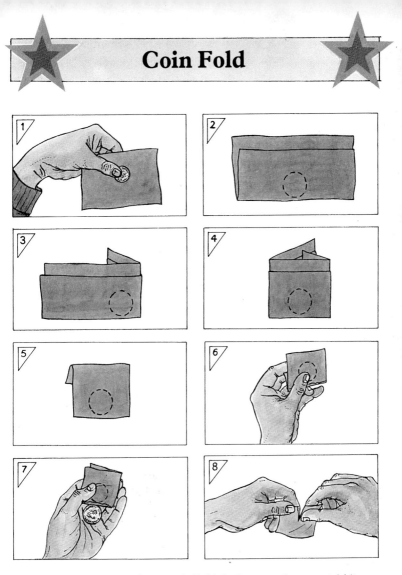

Place a coin on a square of paper (1). Fold the bottom edge up to within one centimetre of the top (2). Fold both sides back (3) and (4).

Fold the top centimetre back (5). The coin appears to be securely held in the packet, but the top edge is open. Turn the packet over so that the open edge is at the bottom (6).

With a pencil tap the packet to prove the coin is still there. Now allow the coin to slip out of the packet and into your hand (7). Tear up the packet – the coin has vanished (8).

The French Drop

Show a coin between the thumb and first finger of the left hand (1). Keep the remaining fingers closed loosely and naturally. Bring the right hand over the top of the left (1a). Place the fingers above the coin and the right thumb below. Start to close the fingers of the right hand. At the same time release your grip on the coin so it falls into the left hand (2). As the fingers of this hand are held closed together the audience cannot see this movement. Continue closing the right hand as though removing the coin from the left.

Move the right hand away from the left and turn it, still in a fist, so that the fingers are uppermost. Do not move the left hand until the right is turned over. Now turn the left hand (concealing the coin) over so the palm faces the floor and use the first finger to point at the right hand (2a). Look at the right hand as you do this.

Move the right hand further to the right. Allow the left hand to fall casually to your side. Do not make a special movement out of this. Concentrate on the right hand. It is supposed to contain the coin. When all attention is on the right hand you should have ample opportunity to drop the concealed coin into a convenient pocket.

Make a crumbling motion with the right hand and open it slowly, finger by finger to reveal that the coin has vanished.

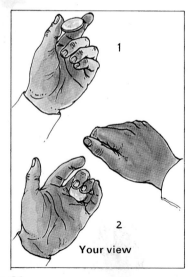

Your view

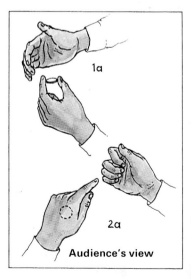

Audience's view

A Natural French Drop

Although the French Drop is a classic SLEIGHT and can be used to vanish a wide variety of small objects it has one drawback. It does not look very natural. Learn the French Drop because you will find it a useful thing to know. But try this more natural version as well.

This time hold the coin in your left thumb and finger but with the coin flat against the finger (1). This is a more natural position than that used in the French Drop. Do not tell the spectators what you are going to do.

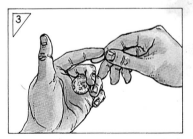

Bring the right fingers towards the coin. The first and second fingers go in front of the coin, concealing it from the audience's view, the thumb goes behind it (2). Secretly drop the coin from the left fingers into the left palm (3). Remove the right fingers as though holding the coin and draw the attention of your audience by asking them to keep an eye on 'this coin'. Look at the right hand as you say this (4).

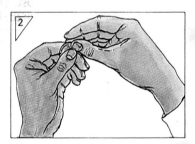

Move the right hand towards the spectators as if offering them a better view of the coin. At the same time allow the left hand to fall naturally to the side. Put the coin in a convenient pocket.

The right hand now places the imaginary coin on your left palm as you ask your audience again to watch closely. Close the left hand around the imaginary coin. Allow the right hand to be seen empty. Pause for a second or two. With the right forefinger point at the left hand. Slowly open the fingers of the left hand. The coin has vanished much to the amazement of your audience.

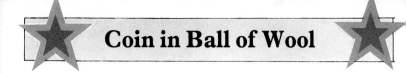

Coin in Ball of Wool

Once you have learnt how to vanish a coin, try this method of producing it from a ball of wool. It gives a coin vanish a dramatic finish.

Equipment: A coin, a ball of wool, a glass tumbler, a flat tin tube just large enough for the coin to slide easily through it.

Preparation: Take the tube and wind the wool into a ball around one end of it (see below). Place the ball of wool, with the tube sticking out of it, into your jacket pocket.

Performance: Vanish a coin by either of the methods given on pages 54–55 or 56–57. The hand that conceals the coin goes into the pocket, drops the coin into the slide, pulls the slide out of the wool (leaving it in the pocket), and brings the wool into view. Put the wool into the tumbler. Do not show that the other hand (or the paper – if you are using that method) is empty. Move well away from the tumbler. Now open your hand (or tear up the paper) and show that the coin has vanished. Ask a spectator to pull the end of the wool and allow the ball to unravel. When he reaches the centre of the ball the coin tinkles out.

As only one coin is used in this trick it is a good idea to have it marked in some way (with a pencil) or its date noted so that the audience appreciate that the coin you produce in the wool is the very same one that was vanished earlier.

Coin slide

Slide in ball of wool

Soapy Secret

Equipment: A handkerchief, a small coin, soap.

Preparation: Rub a piece of soap on one corner of the handkerchief to leave a small amount of soap on the material.

Performance: When someone asks to see your latest trick take the handkerchief from your pocket and lay it out flat on the table. The soaped side should be facing up but as only a small amount of soap is used it will not be seen. The soaped corner should be at the bottom

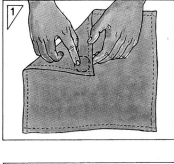

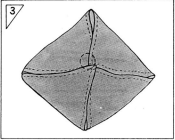

right-hand corner, that is, one of the corners nearest to you. Place a small coin on the centre of the handkerchief.

Put the soaped corner of the handkerchief on to the coin (1) and then place the other three corners on top of this (2) and (3). Press your fingers on the coin so that the soaped corner sticks to it although, of course, your audience is not aware of this.

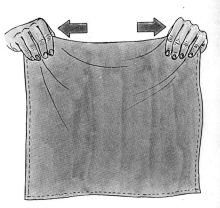

With both hands take hold of the side of the folded handkerchief nearest to you (4). Pull your hands apart quickly so that the left corner of the handkerchief goes into the left hand and right corner (concealing the coin) goes into the right. The coin has vanished!

Coin Escape

Equipment: One fairly large coin, one handkerchief.

Hold the coin between the thumb and first finger of your left hand. Drape a handkerchief over the coin (1). Grasp the coin, through the material, with your right thumb and forefinger (2). Lift it a little and then replace it in the left fingers.

Unknown to your audience, however, there is a slight change in position. As you replace the coin in the left fingers, you secretly obtain an extra fold of material between the coin and your left thumb (3) and (4). It is upon this move that the success of the trick depends.

Now lift the front edge of the handkerchief well over the coin and drop it so that it falls on the other half of the handkerchief which is resting on your left wrist (5).

The next move is simple and yet rather subtle. Simply move your

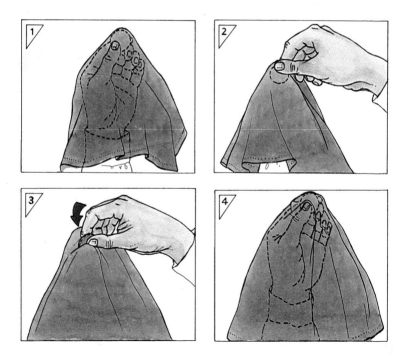

left hand forwards and over so that the thumb is facing the floor (6). This move brings the coin outside and to the back of the handkerchief.

Turn the left hand over slightly and with the right hand twist the handkerchief below the coin so that its shape can be seen through the material. The edge of the folded handkerchief is curled over the top of the coin and to the audience the coin seems to be trapped securely (7). Hold the handkerchief at the twist with the left hand to keep it from unwinding. With the other hand pinch the top of the coin a few times gradually pulling it up and out of the material. It should look as if the coin is penetrating the cloth (8).

Pull the coin out completely and quickly open out the handkerchief to show there is not a hole in it. Because this trick can be performed with items borrowed from a spectator it is well worth learning.

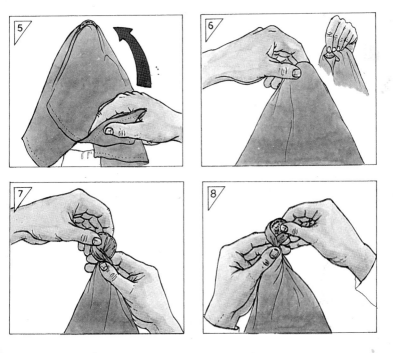

Dissolving Coin

A borrowed coin is dropped into a glass of water. Everyone hears the coin enter the glass and a spectator confirms that it is there. But the coin then vanishes.

Equipment: A coin, a glass tumbler half full of water, a handkerchief, a rubber band.

Performance: The tumbler of water is held on the palm of the left hand. The coin covered with the handkerchief is held by the thumb and first finger of the right hand. Hold the coin over the water and drape the handkerchief over the glass.

You now allow the coin to drop but before doing so you secretly tilt the glass backwards so that when the coin drops it hits the side of the glass and falls into the left hand (1).

Move the glass so that it rests on top of the coin. You can now lift the handkerchief and allow someone to look down into the water. It appears that the coin is in the glass (2).

Cover the glass again and lift it with the right hand (3). As it is covered by the handkerchief the audience thinks the coin is still there. The left hand goes to a pocket to get the elastic band and secretly drops the coin into the pocket.

Place the band around the mouth of the tumbler and put it down on a table. When you get someone to remove the band and the handkerchief, the coin has disappeared. During this action there is plenty of time for you to deposit the coin somewhere else, ready to be 'discovered' a few moments later.

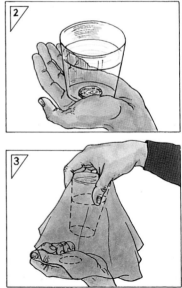

Travelling Coin

Equipment: Two coins.
Performance: Show a coin on the palm of each hand. The positioning of these coins is important. The one on the left hand should be placed below the third and fourth fingers. The one on the right hand should be near the base of the thumb (see diagram 1). Hold the hands palm up about 30 cm (12 in) apart on a table top.

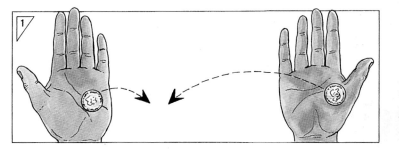

At exactly the same moment turn both hands over so that the thumbs come close together and then draw apart immediately. Your audience will believe there is one coin beneath each hand. In fact, thanks to the original positioning of the coins, the coin from the right hand has been thrown to the left. Although it happens automatically you should still practise the move to get the timing right.

Lift the right hand to show that the coin from that hand has gone. When you lift the left hand both coins are seen to be there, much to the surprise of your audience.

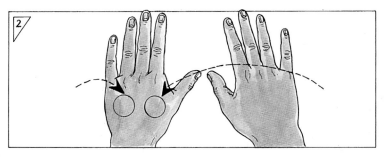

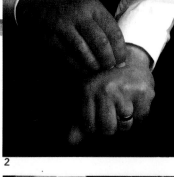

1

2

3

4

Equipment: A coin.

Performance: Show your left hand empty and then close it into a fist. Hold it with the back of the hand uppermost. Show a coin between the fingers and thumb of the right hand and press the coin firmly against the back of the left hand (1).

Move the right hand back and forth as if trying to push the coin through the left hand. As you press down allow the coin to slip behind the fingers of the right hand (2).

Remove the right hand as if you have accomplished your task. Open your left hand (3), and look very surprised that the coin is not there. Say something like: 'I didn't press hard enough. I'll try again.'

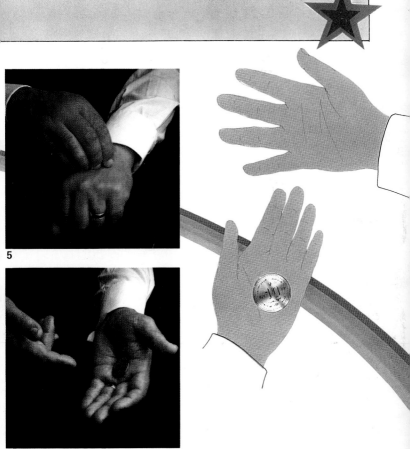

5

6

Close the left hand, turn it over, and bring the right fingers on to the back once again. What your audience does not see is the coin dropped secretly from your right hand into the left just before you close the left hand (4). Look at your audience as you do this and they will automatically look at your face and away from your hands. It is important to do this to prevent the secret move from being spotted.

The rest is just acting. Rub the back of the left hand until you are satisfied that you have 'pushed the coin through the flesh' (5). Show your right hand empty as you open your left. There, resting on the palm, is the coin (6). It must have passed through the back of your hand!

Equipment: A metal disc about the size of a coin with a small hole in it, a short length of cotton, a top hat or other container.

The production of coins from the air is a trick known to magicians as the Miser's Dream. Here is a method by which you can perform this fascinating effect. You can use a real coin for this trick but in most countries it is illegal to spoil coins by making holes in them. Thread the cotton through the hole and tie it into a loop. Loop the cotton on your thumb and the coin will hang down on your palm. By jerking the hand upwards and catching the coin at the fingertips you can make it appear that you have caught a coin from the air.

Carry the coin to a hat and pretend to drop it inside. All you really do is open out the hand and allow the coin to return to its original position. Repeat the above moves several times but vary your position as you produce each coin – pluck coins from the air, from behind your knee and so on.

▲ **Producing** a shower of coins into a container as a finale to this trick.

An Additional Move

It is important that the audience actually 'hears' the coins land in the container. Have a pile of coins on your table (hidden behind something) before you start. Secretly pick up the coins in your left hand as you lift the container with the right. Show the container empty (keeping the coin in that hand hidden). Place the container in your left hand so your fingers, and the coins they hold, are inside. Each time you 'catch' a coin in the right hand and apparently drop it in the container the left hand releases one of its coins.

66

A GRANDE FINALE

With any production trick it is a good idea to have a grande finale – some movement, action or effect that tells the audience you have definitely come to the end of the trick. To end the Miser's Dream, for example, you could produce a shower of coins from your hand or a large coin – so large that it would be impossible to conceal it in the hand.

To perform either of these finales you will need a holder, a device that keeps objects concealed until they are required for production. Holders can be bought from magic shops but a simple and effective holder can be made at home. Cut off the toe of an *old* sock. Sew elastic round the edges of the hole and with a safety pin secure the sock beneath your jacket or coat at one side. Put the coins, balls or other objects, such as eggs, into the sock and the elastic at the bottom will keep them from falling out. The technical name for objects put into a holder like this is the LOAD.

To achieve a spectacular finale to the Miser's Dream put the large number of coins or the special large coin in the holder which is concealed on your left side. As you produce the last coin with your right hand turn the right side of your body towards the audience. This means that the looped coin must be hanging on the palm side of your right hand and that the back of the hand is facing the audience. When you are in this position the audience cannot see the left hand which falls naturally to your side – in just the position to STEAL the load.

The right hand produces the coin and slowly places it in the hat. As this is the final coin it is a good idea to slip the loop from your finger and let the coin slip into the hat so your hands are free for the next effect.

If you have performed your movements slowly and deliberately for this last production everyone will guess that it is to be the final coin. All attention will be focused on this coin which allows you to steal the load from the holder without anyone noticing.

Now turn to face the front as you move behind the table carrying the top hat into which you have apparently been depositing the coins. Bring both hands up together and produce the load. If this load is a number of coins allow them to trickle from your hands and take a bow as the stream of coins ends. If you are producing a single large coin you will find it more effective to hold it up to the audience in a triumphant gesture of success before taking your bow.

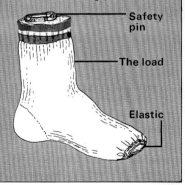

Safety pin

The load

Elastic

Magic with money always interests audiences. This trick has a special appeal for you seem to make money from ordinary pieces of paper.

Equipment: Four banknotes (all the same size), four pieces of white paper (same size as banknotes), glue.
Preparation: Hold all the pieces of paper together (1). Fold the right and left thirds in (2). Fold the top third down (3). Fold the bottom third up (4).

Do exactly the same with the banknotes and then glue the two packages back to back (5). Open out the sheets of white paper. Transfer one sheet of paper from the top to the bottom of the pile beneath the folded banknotes. You are now ready for the performance.

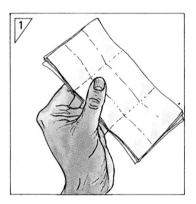

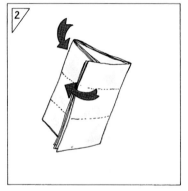

Performance: Hold the papers in the left hand. Take the top paper in the right hand and turn both hands over to show the under-sides of the papers. Because you have a sheet of paper on the bottom of the pile the package of banknotes will not be seen. Show the second paper in the same way, placing it under the paper in

the right hand. Show the third paper but do not turn it over and then place it beneath the first two in the right hand. Show the fourth paper and place it on top of the pile. You will now have the four pieces of paper on top of the still-folded four banknotes (6).

Now fold the papers along the creased lines made earlier. If you

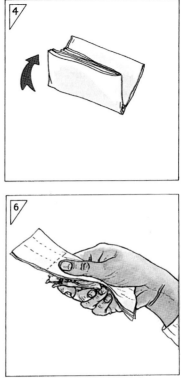

hold everything at waist level the audience will have to look down on to your hands so there is less chance of the package of notes being seen.

Turn the package over and unfold the banknotes. Move the top note to the bottom of the pile and hold all the notes in the left hand. Take the top note in the right hand and turn both hands over. Do the same with the second note. Push the third note under those in the right hand but do not turn it over. Show both sides of the remaining note in the left hand. Place this final note beneath those in the right hand.

Casually fold the package of notes and place them in your pocket as though making money from pieces of paper was the most natural thing in the world.

Magic of the Mind

Mind-reading is one of the most intriguing branches of conjuring. Although it uses many of the principles of magic (and most tricks, with a little thought, can be adapted for mental magic) the audience regards a mind-reader as someone with uncanny powers. They cannot be certain, as they are with conjuring, that the effects are achieved by trickery alone.

There have been many famous mind-reading acts in the past. In the late 19th century, the French magician, Robert-Houdin, performed Second Sight with his son who, although blindfolded, accurately described objects belonging to spectators. In America at about the same time Anna Eva Fay amazed audiences by reading concealed messages. The American Joseph Dunninger was the first mind-reader to work regularly on radio. In the 1920s his performances were billed as 'The World's Greatest Mentalist'. Dunninger worked solo but couples with apparent psychic powers remained popular. The Australians Sydney and Lesley Piddington, for example, convinced radio audiences in the 1950s that they could read minds. Mentalists have also proved popular on television. Al Koran once presented an entire series featuring mysteries of the mind, and the shows of the American mentalist, Kreskin, have been transmitted all over the world.

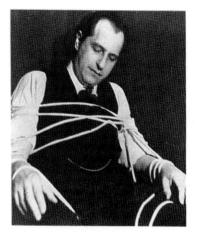

Performing Mental Magic
As with all other forms of magic, you should present mental magic in a way that suits your personality. You could choose to take a very serious approach or make it humorous. To start with, one of the best methods is to pretend that you have no idea why these strange things happen to you.

▲ **Joseph Dunninger** astounded American audiences with mental and psychic effects.

▶ **David Devant** (1868–1948) presenting a thought-reading effect with his sister Dora.

70

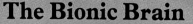

The Bionic Brain

Equipment: Three large cards, red, green and yellow paint or felt-tipped pens, one large envelope, one small envelope, a slip of paper.

Preparation: First make the three large cards. On the first card paint a red spot, on the second a green spot, and on the third a yellow spot. On the back of the red card write 'This is the colour you will choose'. On the backs of the other cards write 'You will not choose this card'. On the sheet of paper write 'You will choose the green card'. Put the paper into the smaller of the two envelopes and seal it down. On the front of this envelope write 'You will choose the yellow card'. Place the small envelope inside the large envelope and seal it down. Place the large envelope flat on your table.

Performance: Although very straightforward to do, this trick will require some practice and you will have to be a good actor to do it well. Show your audience the three cards. Do *not* show their backs. Ask someone to choose any one of the three colours. Allow the spectator to change her mind if she wants to.

This is how you prove you knew which card she would select. Your method of revealing this information depends upon

which colour has been chosen. If red is chosen, do not mention the envelope. Turn the yellow and green cards around to show the messages. Then turn the red card around and the trick is over.

If yellow is the chosen colour, pick up the large envelope and say, 'I guessed you would pick yellow.' Open the envelope and take out the small envelope. Show the message written on it.

If green is the chosen colour, you pick up the large envelope, take out the small envelope (with the message side towards you so the audience cannot see it), and from the small envelope bring out the slip of paper. Drop the envelopes on your table as you

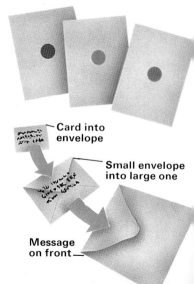

Card into envelope

Small envelope into large one

Message on front

72

say, 'I knew you would pick green and that is why I wrote the colour green on this slip of paper before the show.' Show the paper to prove that you are correct.

In this way whatever colour is chosen you can apparently prove that you knew what would happen even before the spectator had made up her mind!

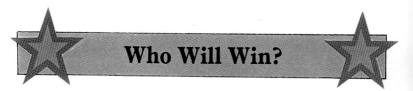

Who Will Win?

Equipment: One banknote, four slips of paper (same size as the note), five envelopes.

Preparation: Put the note (the more valuable the better) in one of the envelopes and seal it down. Mark this envelope with a small pencil dot so you know which one it is. Put the slips of paper into the other envelopes and seal them down.

Performance: Show the envelopes to your audience and explain that one of them contains some money and you are going to give them a chance to win it. Hand the envelopes to someone to mix them up. When you get them back you mix them up some more. What you are really doing is looking for the marked envelope (with the money inside). Mix the envelopes until the marked one is second from the top of the pile.

Hand the envelopes to a spectator and tell him to spell the word 'magic', transferring one envelope from the top to the bottom of the pile as he calls out

each letter. He is to keep the envelope that falls on the letter C. He then hands the envelopes to another spectator who does exactly the same. Two other people also have a go and the last envelope is handed to you.

To make your audience laugh at this point you can do the spelling routine as well but as you have only one envelope it looks rather funny.

Each spectator then opens his or her envelope. But all they contain are slips of paper (you could write some funny remarks, such as 'That's the easiest money you have never earned!' or 'Easy come, easy go' on the slips). When you open your envelope, however, it contains the money. 'It must be magic,' you tell the admiring audience.

⌐Pencil mark

73

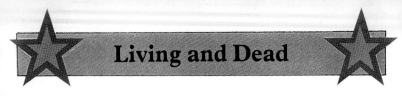

Living and Dead

Equipment: Five plain postcards, five envelopes, five pencils.
Preparation: Mark one envelope with a pencil dot in each corner.

This is a favourite trick of many mind-readers and there are literally
hundreds of different methods used. Five spectators are handed a
postcard, an envelope, and a pencil. Note who has been given the
'marked' envelope and ask him or her to write the name of a famous
dead person on their card and insert it into the envelope. The other
four are asked to write the names of famous living persons. All the
envelopes are sealed and mixed together before being passed to you.
Feeling each envelope in turn, you eventually find the marked
envelope and hold it up in front of you announcing that it contains
the 'dead' name. The envelope is opened and you are correct!

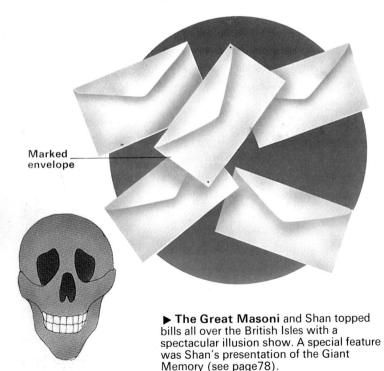

Marked envelope

▶ **The Great Masoni** and Shan topped
bills all over the British Isles with a
spectacular illusion show. A special feature
was Shan's presentation of the Giant
Memory (see page 78).

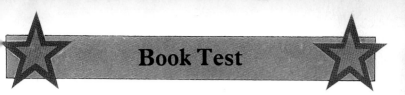

Book Test

Equipment: A book of 150–200 pages, paper, a pencil, lexicon (alphabet) cards, glue or adhesive.

Preparation: On the piece of paper write all the page numbers over one hundred and next to each number the first word of each page. Stick the paper on to the first card in the lexicon pack.

Performance: Hand the book to a member of the audience. Now ask three people each to call out a number so that a three-figure number is arrived at purely by chance. This number must be less than the number of pages in the book, for you now ask the first person to turn to that selected page number and look at the first word on the page.

You now remove the pack of lexicon cards from your pocket. As you fan through the cards looking for the appropriate letters glance at the list stuck to the first card and look up the appropriate word. Remove the cards in the correct order and place them face up on a table to spell the correct word.

Ask the spectator to *think* of his word as you find the letters and you will find that people will later forget all about the book. 'She just asked someone to think of a word,' they will say to their friends, 'And she read his mind!' It is not *what* you do but what people *think* you are doing that is important in mind-reading.

What's Your Name?

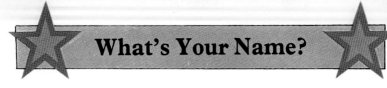

Equipment: Five plain postcards, five pencils, five envelopes.

Preparation: Secretly put a pencil dot on each envelope. Each dot is in a different position, as shown in the illustration, so that you can identify which envelope is which. Mentally number them one to five and put them in numerical order.

Performance: Choose five members of the audience and hand to each a postcard, a pencil and an envelope. As you do so mentally number each person, and make sure that you give envelope number one to person one, envelope two to person two, and so on. Ask each of the five to write his or her name on the card and then seal it in the envelope. Another spectator collects the envelopes and mixes them up before handing them to you.

When the envelopes are returned to you all you have to do is look for the secret mark and you know to which person it belongs. The rest is just acting.

Hold one envelope to your forehead as if concentrating. Then tear it open and hand the card to the appropriate person. It is the card bearing his name! This is then repeated with the remaining four envelopes – and each time you are correct.

One Ahead

The 'one-ahead' principle is used in many 'mental' tricks. As its name suggests the performer is always one step ahead of the audience.

Equipment: A plain postcard, a pencil, a pack of playing cards.

Hold up the postcard showing the numbers 1, 2 and 3 written on it. Ask a spectator to think of a town anywhere in the world. Say you know the town he's thinking of and will write it down. In fact, you write 'Six of Clubs' in the number 3 position on the card (do not let the spectators see what you have written). Ask the spectator the town of which he is thinking. When he tells you glance at the card and say, 'Good,' or something similar.

Now ask a second spectator to think of any four-figure number and you write on the card in the number 1 position the name of the town that the first person thought of. Ask the second person the number of which she is thinking? Whatever she says – frown as though you have made a mistake.

Now write that number against the number 2 position (but put down *one* figure incorrectly – so if the number was 6319 write down 6349 or something

similar). Place the card on the table and move away as you pick up a pack of cards and FORCE a third spectator to select the Six of Clubs (see pages 136–137).

Ask someone to pick up the postcard on the table to check your predictions. Point to the first spectator and ask him what town he thought of. It is the same as your prediction for number 1. Do the same for the number – you are almost correct. The third prediction is called out and the third spectator is requested to reveal, for the first time, the card he selected. And once again your prediction is correct!

The Giant Memory

Equipment: A blackboard or paper, chalk or a felt-tipped pen.

One by one members of the audience call out the names of ten objects which you write on the board against the numbers one to ten. The board is then placed where you cannot see it and yet you can immediately give the correct number for each object, the object at each number, call the objects out in their correct order and, as a finale to a convincing demonstration of your fantastic memory, call out all the objects in reverse order!

There is no trickery involved in this demonstration and the same principle can be used to memorize any list of objects such as shopping lists, or a list of facts for an examination. First you must learn thoroughly the following key words: you will see that they rhyme with their paired number which makes them easy to remember.

1. Bun 2. Shoe 3. Tree 4. Door 5. Hive 6. Sticks 7. Heaven 8. Gate 9. Mine 10. Hen.

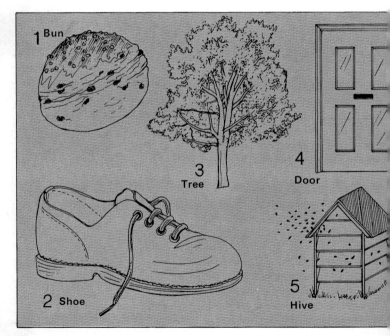

As each object is called you form a mental picture of the object with your key word for that number. For example: if someone shouts out 'glue' for number one you could imagine eating a bun and getting your teeth stuck together. Make your mental picture as funny as possible and it will be easier to remember. Form this picture in your mind while writing the word 'glue' on the board and when you are ready ask for the next object. With each object in the list you form a mental picture connecting the object with the appropriate key word.

When you have written down ten objects the board is turned away so you cannot see the list. Then you ask people to call out any number from one to ten. As soon as the number is called, think of the key word for that number: the picture that you formed will pop automatically into your mind, and you can say what the object is. If an object is called, think of the picture and that will give you the key word which tells you the number. As a finale, run through the numbers both forwards and backwards calling out the objects.

6 Sticks

8 Gate

9 Mine

7 Heaven

10 Hen

Half and Half

The mentalist steps forward with a large sheet of card along the outer edges of which are playing cards with their backs to the audience. The mentalist writes a prediction on his side of the board and then allows a spectator a free choice of any of the cards. This is put into a clip on the top of the board. The board is turned round. The selected card matches the prediction written on the board and all the other cards are different.

Equipment: A large stiff sheet of card, two big elastic bands, playing cards (including ten cards of the same suit and value – the FORCE cards), a felt-tipped pen, one large Bulldog clip, glue.

Preparation: You will need to make ten special cards for this trick. Make them by cutting ten indifferent cards in two (about two-thirds, one-third). These indifferent cards are cards of different values and suits to the force card. Let us imagine the force cards are all the Ten of Hearts. Discard the 'two-thirds' and glue the 'one-thirds' on to one end of each of the force cards so that you now have ten cards with the Ten of Hearts at one end and one-third of another suit and value at the other as shown in the illustration. The *exact* size of the indifferent end depends on the size of the clip you use; read on and you will see why.

Take the piece of stiff card and position the elastic bands along opposite sides. Place the cards face down beneath the bands so that only the indifferent ends of the card show around the sides – the board itself concealing the Ten of Hearts' end (see the illustration). The audience can see the whole of the back of each card. With the clip attached to the top of the board and a felt-tipped pen, you are ready.

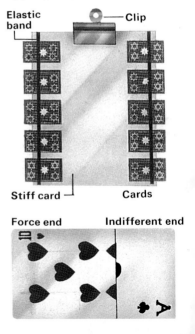

Elastic band — Clip

Stiff card — Cards

Force end   Indifferent end

80

Performance: Write your prediction: Ten of Hearts (how did you guess?) on your side of the board and then ask a spectator to point to any one of the cards that are positioned around the board – make sure that the audience is convinced that the spectator has a perfectly free choice.

As you remove the selected card from its position, allow it to revolve slightly between your fingers so that when you place it into the clip (on your side of the board) the indifferent end of the card is concealed by the jaws of the clip. Whatever you do, do not make a MOVE out of this action. You are a mentalist not a magician and any movements you make must appear to be perfectly natural.

As far as you are concerned the mechanics of the trick are now over. Ask for silence and remind the audience of what has happened so far. Then, quickly, turn the board around. Your prediction is correct, only the force end of the chosen card is visible, and all the other cards are seen to be different.

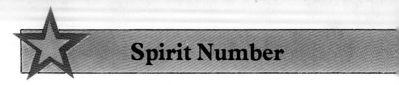

Spirit Number

Equipment: A packet of plain postcards, a wide elastic band, scissors, a small writing pad that looks the same whichever side is uppermost, a pencil.

Preparation: Take a postcard out of the pack and wrap the elastic band around the remainder. On the top postcard write a long number, for example, 1209. Cut the postcard taken out earlier in half and place one half over the number you have just written with its cut end just under the elastic band. Keep the other half for another time. The pack of postcards looks quite ordinary. No one will suspect that the top card is really only half a card.

On one side of the writing pad write three three-figure numbers that will add up to the number

you wrote on the postcard. For example: 324, 593, 292. Use a different handwriting for each number so that they look as if they have been written by three different people.

Performance: Ask a member of the audience to sign his name on the top postcard in the pack. Make sure that he writes on one end of the *whole* card and not on the half card that conceals the previously written number. Turn the pack over and pull out the card on which the spectator wrote his name and hand it to him face down for safe keeping. To prevent him from looking at the card and seeing the number, ask him to sit on it so that no one can tamper with it without him knowing.

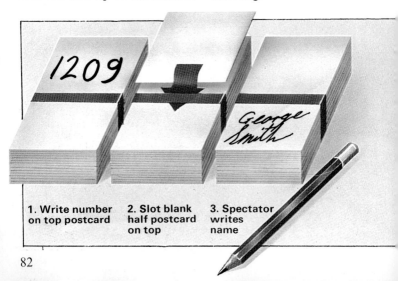

1. Write number on top postcard
2. Slot blank half postcard on top
3. Spectator writes name

Take the writing pad, blank side uppermost, hand a pencil to another spectator and ask her to write any three-figure number at the top. Then ask two other people each to write any three-figure number beneath the first. Do not worry that they will turn over the pad and see your secretly written numbers – they have no reason to do so. And, if you handle the pad naturally, they will not suspect that anything is prepared.

Taking the pad from the third spectator, move across to the other side of the audience, secretly turning the pad over in the process. Ask a fourth person to add up the three *freely* chosen numbers (really the ones you wrote earlier) and announce the total. Reclaim the pad so that the other numbers are not seen accidentally.

Recap what has happened so far, call out the total again, and ask the first spectator to check the postcard he is sitting on. There, above his signature, is the number in question.

ADAPTING THE TRICK

1. The pad can be used to determine the page and line number for a BOOK TEST (see page 75). In the example given the first two numbers 12 could represent the page, and the last two 09 the line. You can either have this line written on a board as a prediction, or pretend to read the spectator's thoughts as he thinks of the selected line.
2. The half-card idea can be used to reveal any information that is known in advance. For example: the name of a selected (forced) card (see pages 136-137).

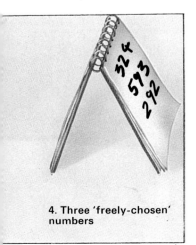

4. Three 'freely-chosen' numbers

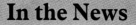

This trick must be performed on a stage with curtains on either side to conceal the presence of a secret assistant.

Equipment: A chair, a strip of cloth long enough to drape over the back of the chair, material to make a pocket, thread, ribbon, a large envelope, scissors, several newspapers and a piece of white card small enough to fit inside the envelope.

Preparation: To go over the chair make a cloth cover with a pocket sewn into the back (see diagram, far right). Put the chair on one side of the stage. String a long ribbon across the stage and hang the envelope (sealed) at the centre. Get your assistant to stand off-stage near the back of the chair in a spot hidden from the audience.

Performance: Invite a spectator on stage and show him several newspapers. Allow him to choose any one he likes and then ask someone in the audience to call out a page number. The spectator turns to that page in the selected newspaper. He is then asked to read out any large headline on that page.

As the headline is announced your hidden assistant back-stage writes it down on the white card and pops it into the secret pocket at the rear of the chair. The chair must be at the extreme edge of the stage so that this action is not seen by the audience or by the spectator helping you.

While your assistant is doing this, draw everyone's attention to the suspended envelope which has been in full view throughout your performance. Explain that in the envelope is a prediction that you made before the show.

To reach the envelope you have to stand on the chair which

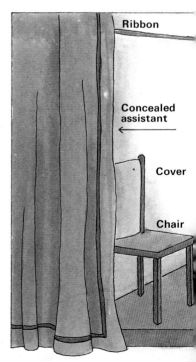

Ribbon

Concealed assistant

Cover

Chair

you bring centre-stage for that purpose. Use a pair of scissors to cut the ribbon. Hold the envelope in your right hand between the thumb and forefinger. As you step down, place your hand on the back of the chair for support. At this point your third and fourth fingers go behind the chair and catch hold of the card. Bring the envelope, with the card held behind it, up in front of your body and use the scissors to cut one end of the envelope. Your right fingers go into the envelope and your thumb rests on the card. Pull the card to the right as if withdrawing it from inside the envelope.

All you now have to do is turn the card over, reveal your prediction to your amazed audience, and take a bow.

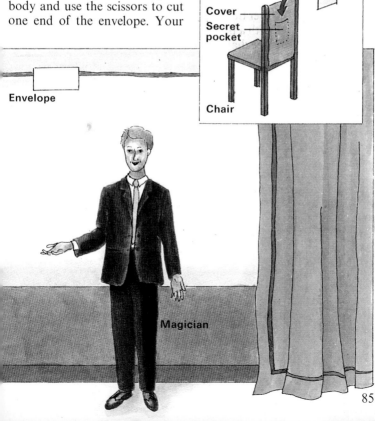

Prediction card

Cover

Secret pocket

Chair

Envelope

Magician

Magic with Rope

The first rope tricks were probably created by accident when people played about with lengths of rope and string. Certainly rope tricks, like most other forms of magic, have been around for a very long time. The Cut and Restored Rope, for example, is described in *The Discoverie of Witchcraft,* written by Reginald Scot in the 16th century, and it was probably in existence long before this.

There is a wide range of rope tricks, and professional magicians often include at least one in their performances. Rope has the advantage of taking up very little room in a case and it weighs very little – an important thing to bear in mind if you have to carry your PROPS from show to show. You can use any soft rope or cord for rope tricks but you will find it much easier to perform with proper magician's rope available from most magic shops (see page 183). You need to have fairly supple hands for rope tricks and to practise your movements thoroughly so that they are relaxed and natural. It is important also to learn how to time each trick – to learn when to make slow and deliberate moves and when to speed up the pace to produce the finale.

Possibly the most famous rope trick of all time is the Indian Rope Trick in which a rope is thrown into the air where it remains rigid. A boy then shins up the rope, but when he reaches the top he disappears and the rope drops to the ground. Unfortunately the trick is nothing but a 'traveller's tale' for magicians have offered large rewards to see just one open-air performance of it, and there have been no takers. Several illusionists, such as Howard Thurston, Horace Goldin and Kalanag, have presented stage versions of the trick.

◀**The Indian Rope Trick** is surely the most famous effect in the whole of magic. Yet it seems to be no more than a traveller's tale. 'Karachi', shown here with his son 'Khydar', claimed to have performed the trick in 1935 but his claim has never been recognized.

87

Quick Knot

Equipment: A rope about 60 cm (23 in) long.

Hold one end of the rope in the thumb crotch of the left hand. Drape the other end over the back of the right hand so that the end portion of the rope lies across the palm (1).

Bring both hands together. Take the left end of the rope above the left hand with the first and second fingers of the right hand (2). At the same time clip the right end of the rope below the right hand with the first and second fingers of the left hand.

Now pull the hands apart and a knot will form in the centre of the rope (3). With practice this can be done extremely quickly.

Simple Quick Knot
(not illustrated)
Equipment: A rope about 60 cm (23 in) long.
Preparation: Secretly tie a knot in one end of the rope.
Performance: Hold the end of the rope (with the knot concealed) in your right hand.

Bring the other end of the rope up into the hand and give the rope a shake. As you shake the rope let go of the knotted end. It appears that a knot has formed in the rope by magic.

88

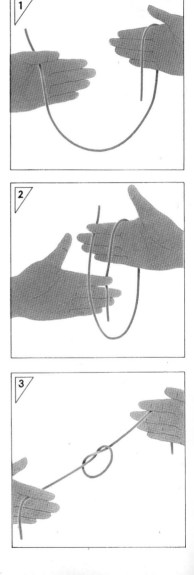

One Handed Knot

Equipment: A rope about 60 cm (23 in) long.

Drape the rope over your right hand. The rope to the back of the hand should be slightly shorter than the part that runs over the palm (1).

Bring the right little finger forward and clip the front part of the rope between it and the fourth finger (2). Start to turn your hand forward so that your thumb will eventually point towards the floor.

As you do this your first and second fingers bend over and catch hold of the back part of the rope just below the hand (3). Give your hand a shake so that the rope falls off the back (4).

As soon as this happens immediately change your finger grip so the rope is held between the thumb and forefinger of the right hand.

With practice you will find that you can do this action so quickly and smoothly that the knot seems to materialize by magic. With even more practice you should eventually be able to do it with a rope in each hand.

Magic Washing

Equipment: Two 3 m (10 ft) lengths of rope, five coloured SILKS, four plastic bangles, weak thread.
Preparation: Put the two ropes side by side and with a short piece of weak thread tie the two together at the centre (1).

Ask for the assistance of two members of the audience. Get one to stand on your left, the other on your right. Take the ropes and show them to your volunteers. Hold one hand over the tied centre so this is not seen. Keeping this centre covered, allow the two spectators to have a mock tug-of-war to confirm that the ropes are strong.

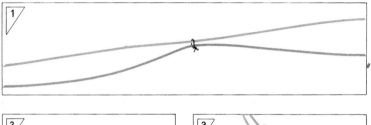

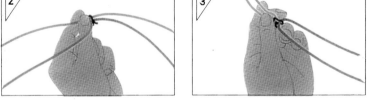

Ask them to drop the ropes and to examine the silks and the bangles to assure themselves that they are free of any trickery. It is during this examination, while all attention is away from your hands, that you make the secret move upon which the success of this trick depends. All you have to do is place your thumb between the ropes on one side of the thread and your second finger between the ropes on the other side of the thread (2). Press your fingers and thumb together and you will automatically move the ropes into the correct position for the trick (3).

Ask one of the volunteers to hand you one of the silks. Still holding the ropes at the middle ask the two volunteers to take up the ropes again. This time, however, (although they are not aware of it) each

person holds *both* ends of one of the ropes. Do not allow them to pull at this stage or they will break the thread. Tie the silk just handed to you around the centre of the ropes. This conceals the join so you now have both hands free (4).

Ask each of the volunteers to thread one of the bangles on the ropes from their end. Tie a silk around the ropes on each side of the bangles. Get them to thread another bangle on from each end. Tie the last two silks around the ropes next to the last two bangles. Push all the silks and bangles towards the centre of the ropes.

Take one rope from each of the two volunteers. Tie the two ropes in a knot on top of the silks and bangles and then hand the ends of the rope back to them (5). Tying this knot has changed over the rope ends so that each volunteer is now holding one end of each rope as they were at the start.

Ask the volunteers to take a firm grip on their ropes and pull sharply. This breaks the secret thread and all the silks and bangles fall to the floor (6). It looks as if they have gone right through the ropes.

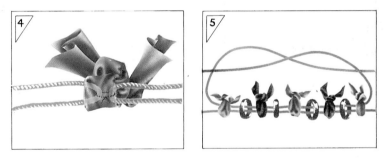

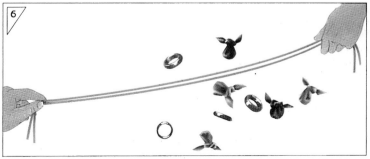

Impossible Knot

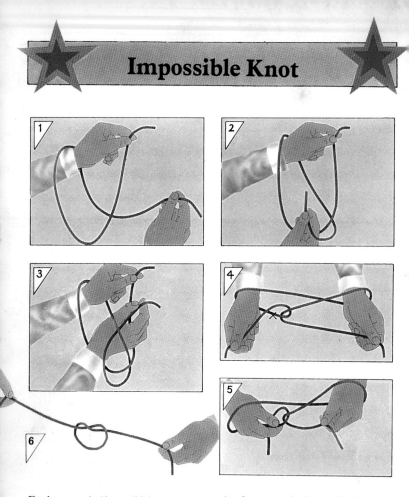

Equipment: A 60 cm (23 in) rope.

Hold the rope at each end between both hands. Bring the right end up behind the left hand and then forward over the wrist (1). There should be a large loop hanging down below the left wrist. The larger this loop, the easier it is to do the moves that follow.

Turn the right hand so the fingers point towards you and then bring the hand closer to your body passing through the loop in the process (2) and (3). Now turn the right hand so

the fingers point towards the audience. At the same time move the right hand up and forwards (4), (5).

It now appears that you simply shake the rope from your wrists. What you actually do is let go of the right end of the rope from your finger and thumb but immediately grasp the rope at the point marked X between your second finger and thumb.

To the audience's surprise there will now be a knot in the rope (6), and yet as far as they know you never let go of the ends.

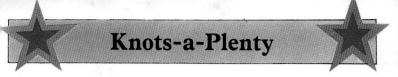

Knots-a-Plenty

Equipment: A rope about 2 m (6 ft) long.

Position the rope so that it lies across both of your hands. Your palms are facing upwards. Move the left hand up slightly, at the same time turning it so that the palm faces towards your body (1). Also at the same time move the right hand up, turning it over so that the palm faces towards you. This forms a loop in the rope.

Place the loop over the left hand and over the end of the rope held by it. As this happens, lift the left thumb to allow the loop to pass, and then return it to its original position.

Repeat the above moves twice more (2) and then carefully lay the rope down for a second. Snap your fingers three times and then slowly lift up the end of the rope. As you lift it up, three knots will form in the rope (3) as if by magic.

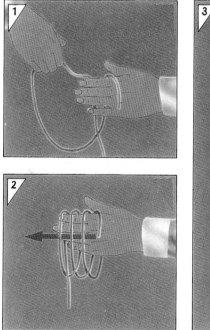

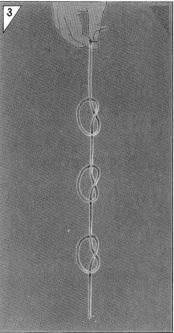

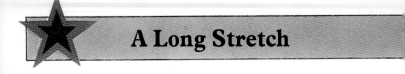
Equipment: One length of rope about 3 m (10 ft) long, two ropes about 30 cm (12 in) long, a rectangular piece of material, two safety pins, a watch.

Preparation: Fold about four-fifths of the material up and sew the sides together to make a bag. Then, following the dotted lines on the diagram below (1), sew in a series of pouches. Thread the long piece of rope through the pouches and pin the bag to the inside back of your sweater or jacket. Take one end of the rope and pull it down the sleeve. Tuck the end of the rope under your watch strap.

Performance: Show the audience the two short pieces of rope. Tie one of the pieces into a loop. Thread the second length through the first

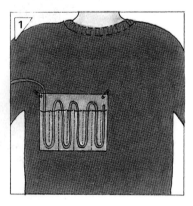

and pretend to tie that into a loop also (2). What you actually do is hold one end of the rope in your hand and tie the other end to the end of the rope that runs up your sleeve (having first released it from your watch strap).

To the audience it appears that the two pieces of rope have been linked together. Hold the loops together and blow on them. Now bring the first loop through the

gap in the second and show the two loops as separate (3). If you reverse the actions you can make the loops 'link' together again.

You now give your audience a shock for you begin to stretch the second loop! In fact you are simply pulling the rope out from your sleeve. Providing you keep the loose end hidden in your hand they will be convinced that you really are stretching the rope.

When the end of the long rope comes down your sleeve you can either stop 'stretching' or gather up as much rope as possible in your hands and then drop most of it to the floor (including the two loose ends). You should now be holding the centre of the rope and you can pretend to continue stretching simply by drawing the rope through your hands.

▲ **This trick,** performed here by the author, makes a dramatic finale to a series of effects with ropes.

FINGER EXERCISES

A magician must have supple fingers to perform tricks especially those with ropes. These two exercises will help to make them flexible. Practise them whenever you can.

1. Touch the end of your little finger with the tip of your forefinger. Touch the back of the finger first then the front.

2. Close your hand into a fist then open the fingers one by one. Start with the forefinger. Repeat the exercise with the little finger, then open the fingers alternately.

Cut and Restored Rope

Equipment: A rope about 1.5 m (5 ft) long, scissors.

This trick may at first sight appear rather complicated. But once you get the idea you will find that it is not as difficult as it may seem.

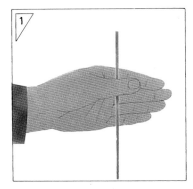

Hold the rope in your left hand (1). Take the bottom end of the rope and place it between the first and second fingers of the left hand (2). Place your right hand on the audience's side of the centre of the rope and then bring the loop back towards your body over the back of your hand (3). Now take the rope at the point marked X and place it between the thumb and forefinger of the left hand (4) and (5).

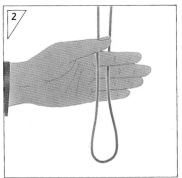

It should look as if you have simply taken the centre of the rope and placed it beneath your

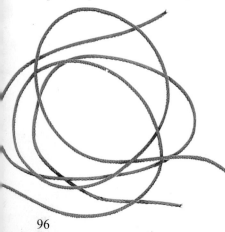

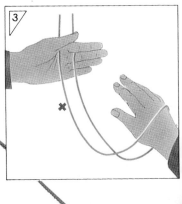

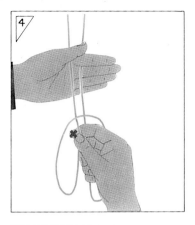

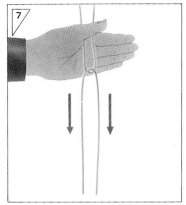

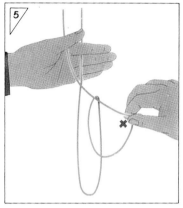

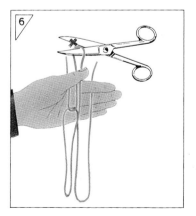

thumb. In fact what appears to be the centre is really just a loop of rope at one end (6).

Take the scissors and cut through the rope at X, allowing the two pieces of rope to the right to fall (6) and (7). The audience now sees what appears to be two pieces of rope of equal length. In fact the ropes consist of a short piece and a long piece linked together.

Bring the end of the right-hand rope up to the top of the short piece (8). Take hold of the short piece in the right fingers (still retaining your grip on the long piece) and move your hand to the right (9) as the left fingers release their hold. It now looks as if the rope has been restored but you are in fact concealing the break in your right hand.

To the audience the trick is over and you should receive some applause at this point.

You now take the trick a step further and apparently tie the

97

two ends together (10). What you actually do is simply tie the short piece around the long piece (11), concealing the two ends of the long rope in your right hand.

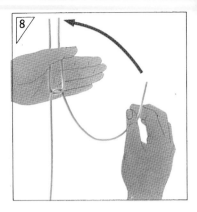

Take the knot in the left hand and pull the right hand to the right (12). The knot slides down the rope but it looks as if you are running the loop of rope through your hands.

Take the scissors once again and pretend to cut the rope. All you really do is place the scissors into the gap in the rope, snip the scissors, and let one end of the rope fall from your hand. It looks as if you have cut the rope in the centre.

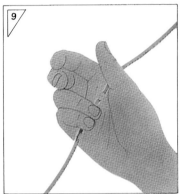

To the audience you now have two lengths of rope tied together with a single knot. You then

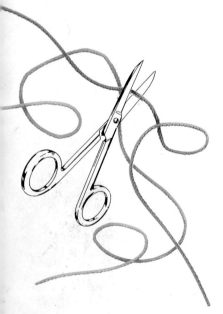

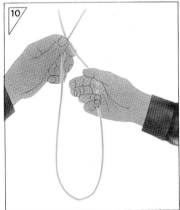

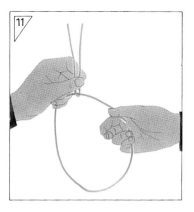

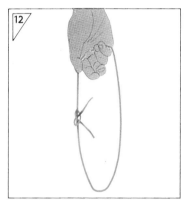

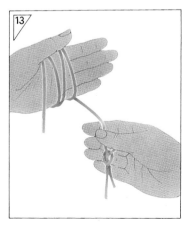

wind the rope around your left hand, allowing the rope to slide through your right hand as you do so. When the right hand reaches the knot just keep on winding but retain the knot in the right hand until it slips off the end of the rope (13). The rope can now be unwound from the left hand and it is seen to be in one piece once again.

You still have the knot concealed in your right hand but it is a simple matter to drop this secretly on your table or into a convenient pocket when you get rid of the rope.

▼ **The sixth stage** in Cut and Restored Rope. Add drama by emphasizing your movements when you perform this trick.

Equipment: Three lengths of rope – one 60 cm (23 in), one 30 cm (12 in) and one 20 cm (8 in) long.

This trick appears rather difficult but if you follow the moves with the ropes in your hand it should be easier to understand. Show your audience three pieces of rope (1). As you show each one in turn, you place the longest (AB) into the thumb crotch of the left hand. The medium length (CD) is placed alongside it between finger and thumb, and the third (EF) is placed slightly to the right of that.

The right hand now brings up the lower end (B) of the long piece and places it in the fingers and thumb of the left hand (2) between the top ends of the medium and short pieces (C and E).

Now lift the lower end of the medium piece (D) and place it to the right of the top end of the short piece (E) – see (3).

Next, see (4), put your right hand through the loop formed by the long piece (AB), take the lower end of the short piece (F) and place it to the right of its other end (E). To the audience you have simply shown three pieces of rope in your left hand and then brought their lower ends up into the hand.

The right hand now moves the three rope ends (EFD) to the right (ends A, C and B remain held in the left hand) and pulls them to the right (5). Because of the way the ropes are linked together it now looks as if all three ropes are the same length. The secret looping of the short length around the long length is concealed in the right hand (6).

To convince the audience that the three ropes really are of the same length, you now count the ropes

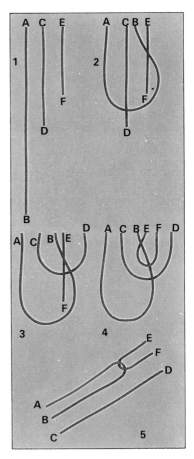

singly from hand to hand. This is how you do it. The right hand takes the medium length rope (CD) from the left hand and moves to the right as you count 'one'. The right hand now moves back and puts the medium length into the left thumb crotch as the right second and third fingers grasp the short and long ropes and move them to the right, 'two'.

On the count of three the right hand removes the medium length of rope from the left hand (7). It appears that you have counted the ropes singly but you have craftily concealed the fact that two of the ropes are linked together. This FALSE COUNT is similar to that used for the Sympathetic Silks described on pages 40-43.

The last rope counted (the medium length, CD) is thrown over the shoulder as you apparently tie the first two pieces together (8). Because of the way in which the ropes are linked all you really do is to tie the short length around the centre of the long length.

Now take the medium length from your shoulder and tie it to one end of the long piece which the audience believes to be two equal lengths tied together (9). You now have what appears to be three pieces of rope joined by two knots.

Now wind the rope around your left hand. The first knot is genuine (A-D) so make sure that it goes into the palm of your left hand. The second knot (F-E) is a slip knot and this is retained in your right hand as you wind the rope around the left hand (this move is exactly the same as used in the Cut and Restored Rope, see page 99).

Draw attention to the rope around the left fist as you casually deposit the false knot from your right hand into a convenient pocket or on to your table. You now unwind the rope from your left hand. Continue unwinding until you reach the knot (10). Take the portion of the rope containing the knot into your

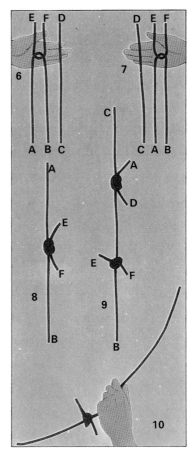

right hand (taking care to keep the knot concealed) and then continue to unwind the rope from your left hand.

Keeping the knot concealed in your right hand, you now display the rope and it looks as if all three ropes have been welded into one.

101

Classics of Close-up

'Close-up', as one would expect, is the term used by magicians to describe the performance of magic with the spectators close to the magician. Audiences tend to think that a magician has to be exceptionally good to perform at close quarters. This is not necessarily true, and in fact there are many instances where it is easier to confuse people when performing close-up.

Many magicians think of close-up magic as a modern development of their art but in fact it is as old as magic itself. Many of the effects described on the following pages are classics which have stood the test of time and proved to be baffling and entertaining over hundreds or even thousands of years. The Cups and Balls is one in particular. There are pictures of this trick being performed at various times all

◀ **The Juggler** by the Flemish painter, Hieronymus Bosch (1450–1516), is the most famous picture of the Cups and Balls. While the attention of the crowd is on the magician a pickpocket steals a woman's purse.

▲ **L'Escamoteur** (the Juggler) of the Chateau d'Eau. This 19th-century print shows a street magician who was popular with the people of Paris. A crowd has gathered to watch him perform his version of the Cups and Balls.

over the world – the earliest shows it over 2500 years ago! There is a 17th century record, too, of a German girl arrested for witchcraft because she restored a torn handkerchief. The trick, Torn and Restored – a version of which is included in this chapter – was probably performed even earlier than this.

Close-up tricks are more widely appreciated today because of television magic shows. Try to learn at least one to include in your magic performances – you may find it one of the most entertaining and popular tricks of your repertoire.

Ghostly Pin

Equipment: A handkerchief, a large safety pin about 5 cm (2 in) long.

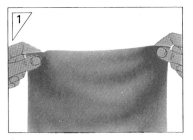

In this trick a pin appears to pass through a handkerchief. Ask for the loan of a handkerchief and get a spectator to hold one corner with his right hand while you hold the next corner with your left hand (1).

Open the pin and push the prong into the handkerchief about 1 cm ($\frac{1}{2}$ in) from the top and near the spectator's hand (2). Close the pin and hold it at the end. Allow everyone to see that the pin really is through the handkerchief.

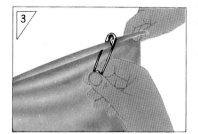

Stretch the handkerchief tight. Lift the end of the pin until it is parallel to the top edge of the handkerchief. This causes the top of the handkerchief to fold over a little (3).

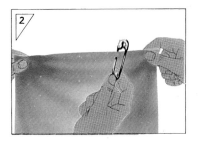

Now push the pin upwards a little. This causes the point of the pin to move slightly but not enough to open the pin. Quickly pull the pin along the edge of the handkerchief (4). At the end of the sweep push the pin forward and back through the cloth (5).

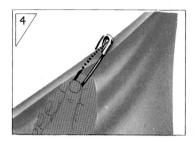

The spectators will think that the handkerchief must have been ripped but it is completely unharmed. Because of the way the pin is held and the fact that the prong is slightly open, the material slides through the head of the pin. The slight fold in the top of the handkerchief conceals this from the audience.

If the pin is not held correctly, the handkerchief will tear so make sure you practise this thoroughly in private before trying it out on someone else's handkerchief.

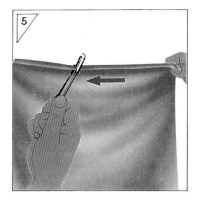

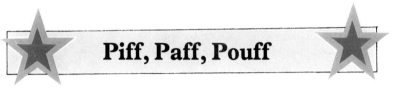

Piff, Paff, Pouff

Equipment: Two large safety pins.

Show your audience the two pins and then link them together (1). Hold the base of one pin in the left hand and the head of the second pin in the right hand. The uppermost bar of the second pin should be held close to the head of the first pin.

Give a secret word or blow on the pins and pull the pins apart with a definite downward movement of the right-hand pin (2).

This movement actually opens the first pin for a moment to release the second pin. But because it happens so quickly the audience is not aware that the pin has been opened and it appears that one pin has melted through the other by magic (3).

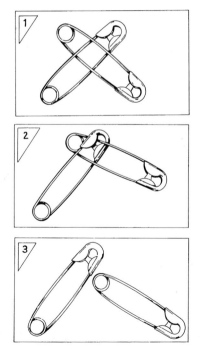

105

Coins Through Table

1

3

This effect is very popular with magicians and lots of routines have been described in magic books. This one is quite simple to do but great care has to be given to the timing of each move to achieve the best impression. You need to be seated at a table.

Equipment: Four coins

Performance: Show your audience the four coins resting on the right hand. Make sure that the lowermost coin is positioned between the first and third joints of the two middle fingers (1).

Tip the coins into the left hand but as you do so bend the two middle fingers in to trap the last coin (2). This position is known as a FINGER PALM. The audience believes there are four coins in your left hand. In fact there are only three as the fourth coin is in the right finger palm.

Place the right hand beneath the table. Bring the left hand down on to the table top, opening the hand as you do so.

Lift the left hand to show three coins on the table and that your left hand is empty (3). Pick up the three coins in the left hand but position the last coin so that it is

held between the base of the thumb and the fingertips (4). In this way it is held outside the fist.

Bring the right hand up from beneath the table and drop the coin it has been holding on to the table. It appears that one coin has passed through the table. At precisely the same moment that the right hand moves forward to drop its coin, move the left hand back towards the rear edge of the table. As the right hand drops its coin on to the table the coin held outside the left fist is casually dropped on to your lap (5).

Now move the left hand back towards the centre of the table as the right hand picks up the single coin. Put the right hand beneath the table. Slap the left hand on to the table and then lift it to reveal only two coins (6).

Pick up the two coins in the left hand, positioning one of them into the crotch of the thumb – the THUMB PALM (7).

4

The right hand now picks up the coin from your lap and it is brought above the table to show that it contains two coins. Pick up the two coins in the right hand and place it beneath the table once again.

Slam the left hand down on to the table but release only one coin, retaining the other coin in the thumb palm. Immediately

5

6

bring the left hand to the rear edge of the table and secretly drop the thumb-palmed coin on to your lap (8). Look at the centre of the table as you do this and the spectators will look there also, thus concealing your secret move.

The left hand now returns to the centre of the table to pick up the single coin. This is held between the base of the thumb and the fingertips, the same position used earlier. Bring the right hand up from beneath the table. This hand contains just two coins for you leave the LAPPED coin where it is for the moment.

Now comes a very subtle and deceptive move. As the right hand comes into view, hold the left hand out in front of you

7

about 10 cm (4in) above the top of the table.

The right hand now drops its coins on to the table top from behind the left hand. At precisely the same moment the left hand drops the single coin it is holding and moves away to the left (9). All three coins (two from the right hand and one from the left)

8

9

108

hit the table at the same time giving the audience the impression that all three coins have come from the right hand.

Pick up the three coins in the right hand and then place that hand beneath the table. Keep the left hand closed at this point. Bring the left hand down on to the table top. At the same time bang one of the right-hand coins sharply against the underside of the table.

10

Lift the left hand to show that the fourth coin has disappeared. Bring the right hand up, picking up the lapped coin on the way, and show all four coins on the right-hand palm (10).

You now apparently deposit all four coins into the left hand. What you actually do is to allow the coins to drop from the right palm and on to the right fingers. At the same time close the left hand as if it contains the coins (11).

11

12

Place all your attention on your left hand. Casually place your right hand under the table as if the trick were over. Then, as if an afterthought has suddenly struck you, slam the left hand down on to the table. At the same time bang the coins held in the right hand against the underside of the table.

Lift the left hand to show that the coins have apparently disappeared. Bring the right hand out from beneath the table and allow all four coins to slide from the hand and on to the table top (12).

Ring on Stick

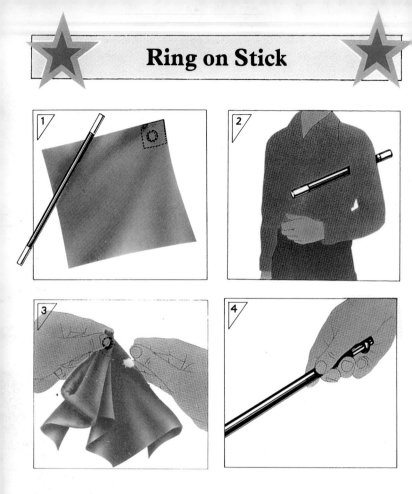

Equipment: A magic wand or a thin stick about 30 cm (12 in) long, a large handkerchief, a plain finger ring.

Preparation: Sew a small pocket into one corner of the handkerchief and place the ring in it (1). Put the prepared handkerchief into a pocket.

Performance: Show the stick to the audience and then place it under your left arm (2). Then ask for the loan of a ring: a plain wedding band is best. Remove the handkerchief from your pocket as you take the ring from the spectator.

You now apparently place the ring in the centre of the handkerchief and then grasp it through the material with the left hand. In actual fact it is the dummy ring in the secret corner pocket that is held by the left hand. The real ring remains hidden at the base of the right-hand second finger (3).

The right hand now removes the stick from beneath the left arm secretly threading the ring on to the stick at the same time (4). This is not easy to do if you are going to avoid the ring and the stick TALKING (making a sound as they touch) so make sure you practise this movement thoroughly before showing the trick.

Tap the stick on the ring in the handkerchief to prove it is there, then ask someone to hold the ring in the handkerchief (5). Do not ask the owner of the ring to do this as he or she might be able to tell that the ring is not the genuine one.

Next you slide your right hand which conceals the spectator's ring to the centre of the stick. Hold the stick horizontally close under the handkerchief and get two more spectators each to hold one end of the stick (6). You can now remove your hand and the ring will remain hidden under the handkerchief.

Take one corner of the handkerchief and pull it from the spectator's grasp. The spectator is under the impression that he was holding the ring right up to the final second but it is now threaded on the stick (7). It appears to have gone through the wood.

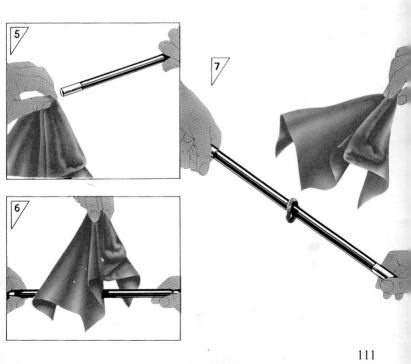

This trick, invented by Paul Curry, is possibly the most amazing effect ever devised with cards.

Preparation: Secretly arrange a pack of cards so that the top two cards of the pack are red cards, the next one is black, then red, then two blacks, then one red followed by 23 blacks and 22 reds (1). You must remember the sequence of the top seven cards.

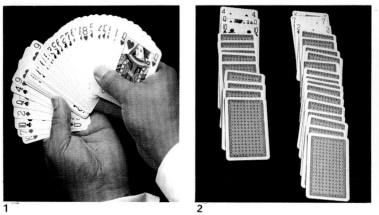

1

Performance: At the start of your performance give the cards a shuffle but use a FALSE SHUFFLE that retains the complete pack in order – see page 140. Do this as casually as you can.

Tell your audience that it is possible to sense the colour of cards without looking at their faces. Remove the top card face down and say it is red. Turn the card over. Continue naming each card's colour before turning it face up (as you have remembered the sequence and the false shuffle has retained all the cards in order, this is not difficult). Place the two colours into separate piles as you deal them.

When you have dealt seven cards, state that anyone can perform this remarkable feat (while saying this give the cards remaining in your hands another false shuffle). Place the pack on the table and ask a spectator to deal the cards into two vertical rows beneath the cards you dealt originally. Without looking at the faces of the cards the spectator has to try to separate the red cards from the black cards. As the spectator is dealing the cards into the two columns you are

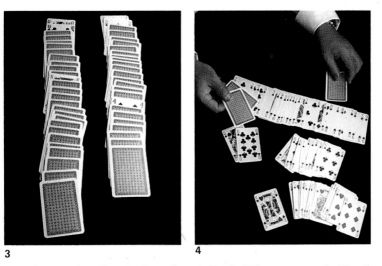

3   **4**

secretly counting the number of cards dealt. When you reach 23 ask the spectator to stop dealing (2).

State that you are now going to change things a little. Remove one of the face-up red cards at the top of the 'red' column and place it face up at the bottom of the 'black' column and place one of the face-up black cards at the bottom of the 'red' column.

The spectator now continues dealing as before but this time placing the cards of each colour he thinks is right beneath the new marker cards you have just set out (3). When the dealing is completed ask the spectator to look at the left column. The cards beneath the black marker are all black, those beneath the red marker are all red (4).

At this point the right-hand column is incorrect. While the first column is being checked you have a chance to change it. Scoop up all the cards from the right column. Now spread the cards face up from left to right until you reach the first marker card (which is face down). Spread the rest of the cards on the table above the ones you have just put down. The marker cards are actually in the wrong place. There are two ways you can overcome this problem:

1. You can ignore it. The effect is so startling that if you casually pick up all the cards, leaving the marker cards face down, it is unlikely that anyone will notice.

2. Another method is to pick up the marker cards and then throw them face down on to the table well away from the other cards. When you pick up the rest of the cards turn the marker cards face up and return them to the pack. No one will be able to remember which card was which.

The Paddle Move

The Paddle Move allows the magician to appear to show both sides of a knife, a book match or a wooden paddle, but, in fact, only one side is shown.

This is how you do it. Hold the handle of a table knife between the thumb and forefinger (1). Turn the hand up and over to show the other side of the knife but, at the same time give the knife a half-turn between the thumb and forefinger (2) and (3). It appears that you have shown both sides of the knife but you have shown only one.

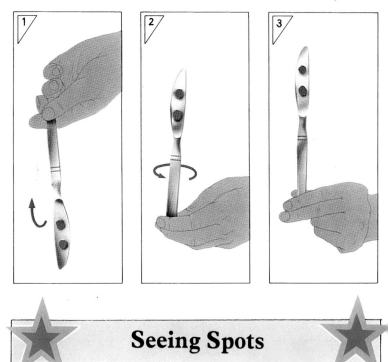

Seeing Spots

This is one trick you can perform with the Paddle Move. First, using saliva, stick four small pieces of paper to the blade of a table knife, two on each side. Show both sides of the knife. In doing this, actually do the paddle move showing one side of the knife only (even though it is possible to show both sides of the knife at this stage). Thus when you do use the Paddle Move later the audience will not be able to notice any difference between it and what appeared to be an ordinary turnover.

With your left hand remove one piece of paper from the knife and pretend to throw it away, actually keeping it in your hand (1). Now do the Paddle Move, but as the knife is turned bring the left hand over the blank space of the original paper and reveal the paper concealed in your hand (2). It should look as if you have again taken a piece of paper off the knife. Now really throw away the paper.

Do the Paddle Move again and show the knife to have one paper on each side (3). In fact there is one on one side and two on the other.

Repeat the above moves, taking away the second piece of paper so it appears that the knife is now blank on both sides. In fact only one side is blank. The other side still has two pieces of paper stuck to it.

Using the Paddle Move show the knife to be blank on both sides. Then, with a quick, upward sweep of the hand, revolve the knife in your fingers to bring the papers uppermost. Do the Paddle Move to show all the papers have returned – two on each side of the knife.

Carefully run your left thumb and forefinger along the blade to remove 'all' the pieces of paper (really only two), place them in your pocket, and you are left with a perfectly ordinary knife.

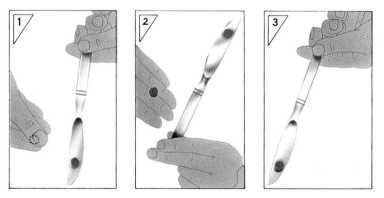

CARD REVELATION

Make a miniature bat out of wood or use a washed ice lolly stick. On one side you write the name of a card you intend to use in a FORCE (see page 136). Have a card selected (forced). Show the bat blank on both sides, using the Paddle Move. Ask what card was selected (as if you did not know!) and slowly turn the bat over to reveal the card's name.

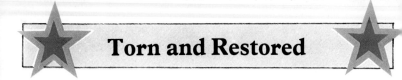

Torn and Restored

The destruction of an object which is then magically restored is a popular theme in conjuring. All you need for this version of the theme is a prepared packet of cigarette papers. It is a good idea to carry this prepared packet with you at all times in case someone asks to see a trick.

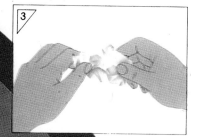

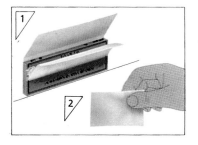

Equipment: A packet of cigarette papers.

Preparation: Take out one cigarette paper, roll it into a small ball, and hide it under the top paper in the packet (1).

Performance: Remove a paper from the packet, secretly holding the rolled-up paper behind it. You will find that the secret paper can be covered quite easily by the thumb so that you can casually show the paper on both sides. Make sure that you hold the paper with finger and thumb only so that it can be seen that your hands are otherwise empty (2).

Tear the paper into pieces, keeping the duplicate paper hidden. Now bring the fingertips of each hand closer together to squeeze the torn pieces into a small ball. Emphasize the squeezing movement, but at the same time bring the 'duplicate' paper into view and allow the torn pieces to be concealed between your finger and thumb.

Ask someone to 'blow on the torn pieces' and then slowly open out the ball of paper (the duplicate piece) to show that it has been restored (3). You are now back to the same position from which you started with a piece of paper showing and a small ball concealed behind it.

Hold the paper still for a few seconds to give the spectators time to appreciate what you have accomplished. Then crumple up the paper (at the same time wrapping it around the torn pieces) and casually put the ball into your pocket.

Performing Torn and Restored

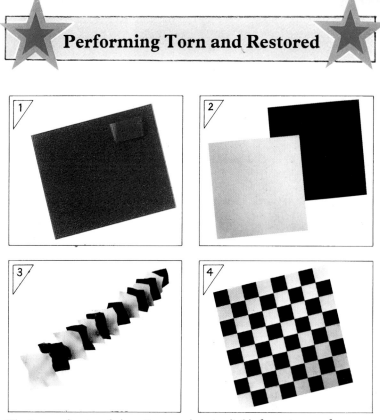

The torn and restored cigarette paper is not suitable for a stage performance because many in the audience will not be able to see what you are doing. Most close-up tricks, however, can be adapted for a stage performance.

The first thing you could try is a simple increase in the size of the paper. Use coloured tissue paper to brighten the effect. The duplicate paper has to be folded rather than crumpled up to make it easier to handle. Glue it to the back of the original sheet (1). But with this method you cannot show the original sheet on both sides as the duplicate will be seen.

Another trick can be made by using two sheets of tissue paper – one black, one white – each about 18 cm (7 in) square (2). The duplicate sheet is made up of black and white squares like a chequer-board.

Show the black and white sheets. Place one on top of the other and tear them up together (3), making the pieces about the size of the folded duplicate so that you have a packet of torn pieces in front of the duplicate. Simply turning the packets over exchanges them. Open out the chequered sheet and say, 'That is how chess boards are made' (4). The trick is made more logical if the chequered sheet is as large as the two original sheets combined.

The Cups and Balls

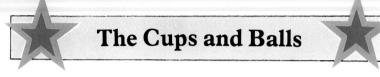

The oldest trick known to magicians is the Cups and Balls. Here is a simplified version that you can try.

Equipment: Three beakers that nest (fit one inside another), four small balls of sponge or screwed-up paper, one large soft ball and a table covered with a cloth.

Preparation: Place the big ball in your left pocket. Put one small ball in each cup and nest the cups together. Conceal the fourth ball in your left hand (1).

Performance: At the start of your performance you put each of the cups upside down on the table. If you do this movement quickly and smoothly the balls will stay in the cups as you turn them over, and the cloth on the table will deaden the sound as each ball drops on to the table top (1) A, B and C.

Tap each cup and lift the first to reveal a ball beneath it. Lift the cup

with your right hand and casually place it into the left, its mouth over the concealed ball, as you direct all attention towards the ball on the table (2). The second and third cups are lifted to reveal two more balls. As you pick up these cups you nest them on top of the one in your left hand.

Place the three cups mouth down, behind each of the balls. The first two cups are placed to the right and left positions and the third cup is placed in the centre (3). There is now a ball under the centre cup because, as you removed the cups from your left hand, you let the concealed ball drop into the last cup. The audience is not aware of the presence of this extra fourth ball.

Pick up one of the balls and place it on top of the centre cup, and then

118

nest the other two cups on top (4). Tap the uppermost cup and lift all three cups *as one* to reveal a ball on the table. It appears that the ball has penetrated the base of a cup.

Once again place all three cups on the table but place the middle cup (containing the extra ball) in the central position over the one ball on the table. Place a ball on top of this cup (5), then repeat your previous actions to make it apparently pass through the base – and reveal two balls on the table when you lift the three cups together.

Do the same again with a third ball but this time step back and allow a spectator to tap the top cup. While he is doing this you have ample opportunity to steal the large ball from your pocket and hold it within

your left fist. Lift all three cups as one to show that there are now three balls on the table and casually place the nested cups into the left hand over the concealed large ball (6). Put all three cups on the table with the large ball concealed beneath the bottom cup. The fourth ball remains hidden between the bottom and second cup. This action should be made casually as if the trick had finished.

As you place the cups on the table pick up the three balls one at a time and say: 'I am often accused of using more than three balls when I do this trick. Against all the rules of magic, I will let you into a secret – I use four. *This* is the extra one.' As you say this, lift all three cups as one to reveal the large ball.

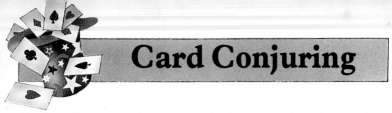

Card Conjuring

Card magic is one of the most popular branches of magic. A pack of cards is familiar to most people all over the world, takes up very little room in one's pocket or case, and yet it can be used for literally thousands of mystifying effects. With a pack of cards you can carry a complete act in your pocket.

Some card tricks call for expert SLEIGHT-OF-HAND, or 'finger flinging' as some magicians call it (particularly those who cannot do it themselves). There have been many expert 'finger flingers' in the past. The great American escapologist, Harry Houdini, once billed himself as the 'King of Cards'. But one of the most impressive card manipulators of all time was Cardini who, in the early 1900s, produced fan after fan of cards from his gloved hands. But finger

▼ **Sorcar** was the greatest Indian magician of all time. From 1955 to 1961 he toured the world with a spectacular illusion show, featuring this large-scale version of the classic Four Ace Trick.

▶ **Paul Daniels** performs one of his famous card tricks with which he has amazed audiences all over the world. His regular television shows feature many top performers.

▲ **Old playing** cards are often very colourful. They were one of the earliest props of the magician.

flinging is not absolutely necessary for the performance of most card tricks. The majority of them are reasonably easy to do as long as they are practised thoroughly first.

Variety is essential in all forms of magic and it is particularly important when conjuring with cards. Most card tricks consist of the spectator taking a card and the magician identifying the card in some manner. Indeed, almost all of the tricks in this section fall into this category. As you will see when you try them, they are all completely different – to a magician that is. To an audience they are all the same trick – the magician locates or identifies a card selected by a spectator. When performing a number of card tricks, therefore, make sure you include as many as possible that are not straightforward location tricks, such as Threes and Fours, Fabulous Four Aces and Out of This World (see page 112).

Whole books have been written on card magic, and even on specific aspects of the art of card manipulation, and this one barely scratches the surface. But on the following pages you will learn some of the basic principles of card magic, principles with which you can entertain your spectators.

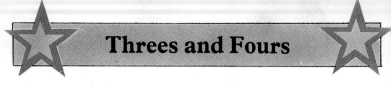

Equipment: A pack of playing cards.
Preparation: Put the four fours on top of the pack and on top of these place the four threes.
Performance: Give the cards a FALSE SHUFFLE that does not disturb the order of the top eight cards – see Retaining Top Stock on page 140. Deal the top eight cards face down on the table in a row and ask a spectator to pick any card.

Push the selected card forward, still face down. Pick up the remaining cards from left to right, tucking each card picked up below the previous one, and place the seven cards on top of the pack. No matter which card remains on the table the order from the top of the face-down pack is several threes (either 3 or 4), then several fours.

▶ **The finale** of Threes and Fours. Spectators should not, of course, be aware that the cards are in any special order so be sure to arrange the set-up for this trick in secret before you show it, never in front of the audience.

Start dealing cards from the top of the pack face down on to the table in one pile. When you have dealt *at least* seven cards ask one of the audience to call 'stop' whenever she wishes.

Stop dealing at the point called. Put to one side the cards left in the hand. Gather together all the cards dealt on the table and hold them in your left hand. Now say you will deal the cards into a number of piles according to the value of the selected card. If the card is a three, deal the cards into three face-down piles. When you turn over the top card of each pile, it is shown to be a three – quite a coincidence! Should the selected card be a four you simply deal the cards into four heaps. The top card of each heap is turned over to reveal that the top four cards are the four threes.

The Red Card

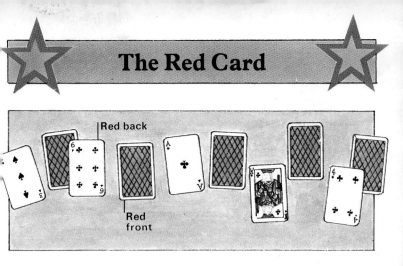

Red back

Red front

Equipment: Eight black cards with blue backs, one red card with a blue back, and one black card with a red back.

Preparation: Arrange the cards in a packet so that when you lay them out they look like the illustration above (the values of the cards do not matter provided that the third card from the left is a face-up black card with a red back and the fourth from the left is a face-down red card with a blue back). On a piece of paper write: 'You will choose the red card' and hand this to someone for safe keeping. At this stage it is important that no one knows what you have written.

Performance: Ask someone to choose any number from one to ten. The number chosen will determine your next move. If the selected number is 1, 2, 5, 6, 9 or 10, *spell* the number from left to right tapping a card for each letter as you do so. For example, if one is chosen, you spell O-N-E

and end up on the third card from the left (the same will happen for the numbers 2, 6, and 10). If you spell F-I-V-E you end up on the fourth card from the left, as will also happen if 9 is chosen. If 3 or 4 are chosen, *count* along the row from left to right. If 7 or 8 are selected count along the row from right to left. In this way whatever number is chosen by the spectator you will end up on either the third or the fourth card from the left.

Now all you have to do is reveal your prediction. If it is the third card turn all the face-up cards face down and it is seen that they all have blue backs. Now turn the third card face down and it has a red back. If the fourth card is arrived at, turn all the face-down cards face up whereupon it will be seen that all the cards are black. Turn the fourth card over and it is seen to be red. Either way your prediction will prove to be correct.

Sim Sala Bim

Equipment: A pack of playing cards.

Performance: Deal out three piles of seven cards each, face down. Ask a spectator to choose one of the piles. Pick up the pile he selects and display them in a fan facing towards the audience – there is no need for you to see their faces. Ask the spectator to choose and memorize any of the cards he sees. He must not tell you which it is.

Place the pile from your hand in between the other two piles, so you now hold a pack of 21 cards. Deal the cards out one at a time into three piles. Pick up each pile individually and display them to the spectator and ask him to indicate which pile contains the selected card (again, the spectator must not name the card in question).

Once again place the pile containing the selected card between the other two piles and deal out the cards one at a time into three piles. Fan out the cards and for the third time place the pile of cards containing the selected card between the other two piles.

You now mention the magic words 'SIM SALA BIM', words which will help you find the card chosen by the spectator.

Pick up the packet of 21 cards and spell S-I-M S-A-L-A B-I-M, placing one card on the table for each letter spelled. Believe it or not, the very next card will be the spectator's chosen card.

▶ **Dante** (Harry August Jansen) toured the world with his magic show Sim Sala Bim (nonsense words from an old Danish song). Dante was born in 1882 and as a schoolboy baffled his friends by making a button vanish. By the time he was 20 he had an hour-long show and he carried on performing until shortly before his death in 1955.

Do As I Do

Equipment: Two packs of playing cards.

Performance: Give a spectator one pack of cards; keep the other for yourself. Both of you shuffle your pack. You now exchange packs and shuffle the cards again. Once again you exchange packs but this time you secretly look at and remember the bottom card before handing the pack to the spectator.

Ask the spectator to remove any card from his pack, look at it, and remember it, and say that you will do the same. Look at the card you have selected but make no attempt to remember it. Each selected card is then placed on the top of its pack and the pack is then cut once. The selected cards are now 'lost' in their packs.

Once again you exchange packs. Each person then fans through this pack and removes the duplicate of the card he chose. In actual fact you do not do this. You really look for the card you saw previously on the bottom of the pack. Because of the way the packs have been exchanged and cut, the card to the right of the one you remembered will be the card selected by the spectator. This is the card you remove, pretending it is your card.

Both you and the spectator hold your cards face down. You then turn them over and they are seen to be identical. What a coincidence!

KEYS or LOCATORS to magicians are specially prepared cards that can be found easily in a pack of cards. There are many types of keys, some of which are described here.

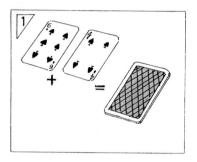

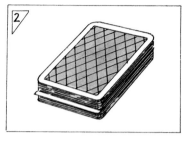

Long Card (2)

This is a card that is slightly longer than the cards in the rest of the pack. Because of this, it sticks out at one end and it is a simple matter to cut the cards at this point.

Thick Card (1)

This is simply two cards very carefully glued together. Place a thick card anywhere in the pack and RIFFLE the cards. As you pass the thick card, you will hear a loud click which means that, with practice, you can cut the cards at this point every time.

Crimp (3)

To make a crimped card simply bend one corner slightly. When this card is placed in the pack it forms a gap (magicians call this gap a break). It is fairly easy to cut at this break every time. Make sure your audience does not spot you making the crimp.

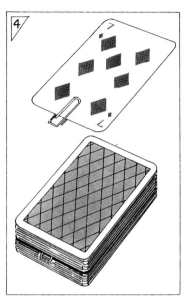

Paper Clip Locator (4)

Place a paper clip on any card and it becomes an instant key card. The paper clip should be at the end of the pack nearest your body, however, or the audience will see the break caused by the clip. It is extremely easy to cut the cards at this key card.

Any Card a Key Card (5)

By secretly making a mental note of the bottom card of the pack before doing a trick you are equipped with a key card. On page 125 you will find a trick using this strategem but there are many other 'miracles' that can be accomplished with this method.

TAKE A CARD – ANY CARD

Knowing about these different types of locator is not enough to enable you to make use of these stratagems. But there are many tricks which use a key card to find a card selected by a spectator. Practise these and keep a key card in your pack – you'll find you can astound your friends.

Equipment: A pack of playing cards, a table.

Preparation: Put a thick card (page 126) anywhere in the pack.

Performance: Give the cards a shuffle and cut the cards so that the thick card is brought to the top of the pack. That is not as difficult as it sounds. If you RIFFLE the inner end of the cards you will hear a definite 'snap' as the thick card passes your thumb. You will also be able to feel it. If you cut the cards at that point the thick card will be on the top. Practise this until you can do it without thinking.

Spread the cards, face down, to allow a spectator a free choice of any card. When he has looked at it, ask him to replace it on the top of the pack (on top of the key card). Pick up the entire pack.

Take the lower half of the pack and shuffle the cards *on to the top card*. Don't shuffle the whole pack. Cut the cards, bringing the thick card to the top once again, and the chosen card will be at the bottom of the pack.

Here is one way to reveal its identity. Hold the cards from above between the thumb and fingers of the left hand so that the face of the bottom card is resting on the fingertips. By moving the second finger back slightly, the bottom card, in this case the chosen card, moves towards the

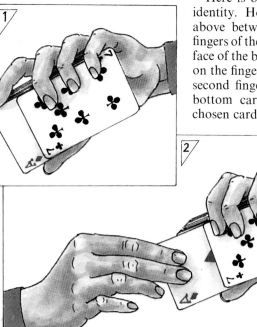

wrist about 15 mm ($\frac{1}{2}$ in). The illustration (1) shows the view from below at this stage. This is known as the GLIDE.

The right second finger is now brought to the underside of the pack to remove the bottom card. But because the bottom card has been drawn back it is the next card that is actually withdrawn (2). Ask the spectator to say when you should stop and go on dealing cards until he calls 'stop'.

Pause for a moment and then withdraw the real bottom card. Hold it face down for a while, as you point out that the selected card was shuffled into the pack, that you drew cards from the bottom one at a time, and that it was the spectator who decided where you should stop. Ask the spectator to name his selected card and then turn the card over on the top of the table. Magic has happened again!

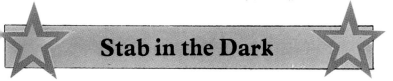

Stab in the Dark

Equipment: A pack of playing cards, a newspaper, a paper knife.

Performance: Have a card selected and returned to the pack. In doing this, crimp the selected card as described on page 126 and 143. The pack can now be shuffled quite fairly but the crimp and the break it forms will always enable you to locate the selected card.

Cut to the break. When you complete the cut the selected card will be at the bottom of the pack. Shuffle the cards to bring the selected card to the top, using the second part of the shuffle described under Retaining Top Card on page 141.

You now show a double page from a newspaper. Hold this in your right hand with the pack in your left hand. Bring the paper over to wrap up the pack. As soon as the paper hides the pack from view turn the pack face up. Continue covering the pack with the paper.

Hand a spectator the paper knife and ask him to thrust the knife through the newspaper and into the side of the pack. Leave the knife in position. As soon as this is done, loosen the paper and reach underneath to take the cards from below the knife. Turn the cards over (face down) before you bring them into view. It appears to the audience that the top (face down) card is the card below the insertion of the knife. Ask someone to take this top card and to reveal its identity. It is the selected card!

To the audience the effect is finished but the cards remaining inside the newspaper are still upside down. Casually reach beneath the paper and turn the cards over before bringing them into view.

Quick Change

A card is selected by a spectator and returned to the pack. Even though the card is buried in the pack, the magician maintains he or she can find it. After running through the pack, the magician removes one card, and places it face down on the table. The magician claims the card is the chosen card, the spectator says no – but it is!

Equipment: A pack of playing cards, a table.

Performance: To do this trick you need to be able to locate a previously chosen card (see pages 126 and 142). Run through the cards and then cut them to bring the selected card to the top.

You now have to lift off the top two cards as one. This is known as a DOUBLE LIFT. One way to do this is as follows. Hold the cards in the left hand. Bring the right hand to the pack. Grip the pack with the thumb at the inner end (nearest your body) and your second finger at the outer end. The right forefinger rests on the back of the top card. Use the ball of the right thumb to lift up the top card and the second card. Continue lifting the two cards with the thumb. Gradually bring the thumb and forefinger together (so the thumb goes on to the face of the card(s)

and the forefinger is on the back) and lift the two cards off the pack together as if they were only one card. Turn the cards over as one card and display the face to the spectator and the audience. Casually replace the cards on top of the pack and immediately deal the top card only on to the table as you say, 'That's your card.'

When the spectator denies it is his chosen card you ask, 'What was your card?' As he names the card, point to the card on the table (you should have moved well away by this time) and say, 'Well, what is *that* then?' The spectator will immediately turn the card over, and to his surprise discover the card has changed to the one he selected!

KEEP THEM TOGETHER

When performing the DOUBLE LIFT it is important that the two cards removed from the pack are kept in perfect alignment – all edges perfectly together. To help you to do this it is a good idea to bend the cards slightly as they are then less likely to spread apart.

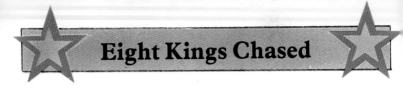

Eight Kings Chased

It is often useful to arrange a whole pack of cards in a secret order known only to the magician. 'Eight Kings' is the name given by magicians to the SET-UP described here. With its aid some surprising and baffling feats are possible, some of which are given on pages 134 and 135.

First you must know thoroughly the following rhyme:

> Eight kings threatened to save
> ninety-five ladies
> for one sick knave

You must be able to recite this (to yourself) without hesitation if you want to use this principle. The rhyme represents the order of the cards as follows:

Eight	Kings	threatened	to	save	nine	ty-five	ladies	for	one	sick	knave
8	King	3	10	2	7	9	5	Queen	4	Ace	6	Jack

That, of course, represents only 13 cards in the pack so you must have a way of remembering the suits. This is normally done by the use of the word 'chased' which represents the suits in the following order:

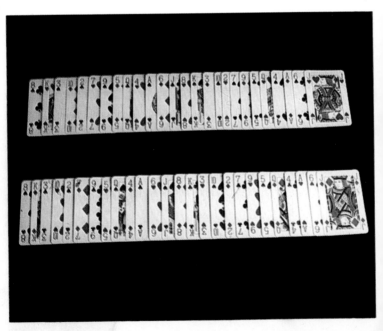

Clubs	Hearts	Spades	Diamonds
C	H	S	D
	a	e	

After using this for a while, you will find that 'Clubs, Hearts, Spades, Diamonds' becomes the natural way to remember the suits and you will no longer need to use 'CHaSeD' as a memory jogger.

To arrange the cards, follow both of these rules and the order of the pack is as shown on the opposite page. A set-up pack must not be shuffled if you wish to keep the order. It can, however, be cut as many times as you wish and the secret order will not be disturbed. Alternatively you can use a FALSE SHUFFLE in which the complete pack is kept in order (see page 140).

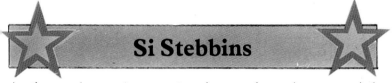

Si Stebbins

Another popular complete set-up is Si Stebbins. In this, the value of each card is increased by three each time. So, if you look at a four you will automatically know that the next card is a seven, and that this is followed by a ten. In this set-up the picture cards are given a numerical value: the Jack is 11, Queen 12 and the King is 13.

Using the 'chased' sequence described under Eight Kings, the order for a complete pack will be as photographed below.

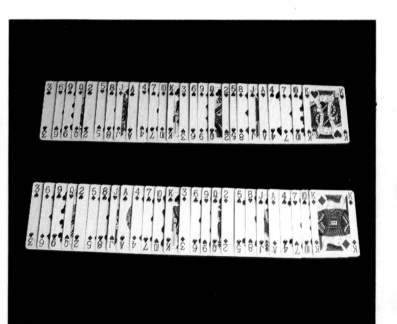

Mental Identification

Equipment: A pack of pre-arranged playing cards (either Eight Kings or Si Stebbins).

Performance: Fan out the pack of cards face downwards, to allow a spectator to remove and keep any card he wishes. Divide the pack at that point and place the upper portion beneath the lower portion as if simply cutting the cards. This action brings the card that was above the 'removed' card to the bottom.

Hold the pack in the right hand and point or gesture to the spectator with that same hand as you say: 'Please concentrate.' You must do this in such a way that you get a quick glimpse of the bottom card. By a simple calculation you can now work out the value of the selected card. If, for example, the bottom card is the Three of Spades the selected card will be the Ten of Diamonds (Eight Kings) or the Six of Diamonds (Si Stebbins).

Now pretend to read the spectator's mind. 'I think you have chosen a red card. Am I correct? Yes, I get an impression of a diamond...' and so on.

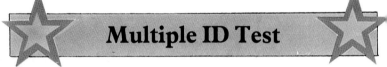

Multiple ID Test

Equipment: A pre-arranged pack of playing cards (either Eight Kings or Si Stebbins), a table.

Performance: Ask three spectators each to remove a card from different parts of the pack and to memorize their selected card. The cards are then pushed back into the pack wherever each spectator wishes.

Cut the cards a few times and then fan them out so only you can see their faces. It is a simple matter to pick out the three selected cards because they will be out of sequence, see opposite.

Place the three cards face down on the table. Ask each spectator to name his card, turn them over and take your bow.

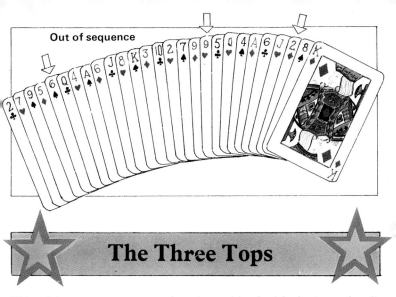

Out of sequence

The Three Tops

This trick uses a pre-arranged pack combined with the 'one-ahead' principle described on page 77.

Performance: Cut the cards a few times. On the last cut secretly look at the bottom card. A simple calculation tells you the value of the top card (let us assume it is the Jack of Diamonds).

Now cut the pack into three heaps (or get a spectator to do it for you). Keep your eye on the final position of the top portion. Tap your finger on one of the other portions and say boldly: 'This is the Jack of Diamonds.' Pick up the top card on that pile and hold it towards you.

Now tap the next pile and state the top card to be the one you are actually holding. So, if you picked up the Seven of Clubs from the first pile, you tap the second pile and say: 'This is the Seven of Clubs.' Once again remove the top card and place it facing you with the first card.

Let us assume that the card you have just picked up is the Two of Spades. This is the card you call as the top card of the third pile (the value of which you have known from the start to be the Jack of Diamonds).

Remove the top card from the third heap and place it beneath the two cards you hold in your hand. Slap the three cards down on the table and it is seen that you have correctly identified all three cards.

If you are careful to replace the three cards on top of the correct piles at the end of this trick and you reassemble the piles correctly the pack will be in the same order as you started.

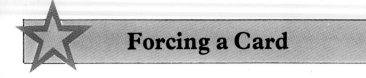

Forcing a Card

The success of some tricks depends on you being able to FORCE an independent and free-choosing spectator to 'pick' a card that you want him to take. On these pages are some forces worth knowing. Once you have learnt how to force a card, you must reveal its identity in a magical way. Turn to pages 138-139 for ideas on how to do this.

Cut Force

The force card (chosen by you) is at the bottom of the pack. Place the pack on the table. Ask a spectator to cut the pack in two and then to place the bottom half crosswise on top of what was the top half 'to mark the cut'. You must now talk for a few minutes to allow the audience to forget the details of what has gone before. Eventually ask a spectator to lift off the upper portion of the pack and look at the 'card he selected' (the bottom card of the top portion – the force card).

Slip Force

The force card is on top of the pack. RIFFLE through the cards requesting that a spectator says 'stop' anytime she likes. When stopped, use your right hand to open the pack like a book at the place selected. Remove the upper portion from the lower at the same time pressing on the top card (force card) with the left fingers. This enables you to remove the upper portion with the exception of the top card which drops on to the top of the lower portion. Offer the lower portion to the spectator asking her to take the 'top card'. The card she has 'selected' apparently from the middle of the pack is, of course, the force card.

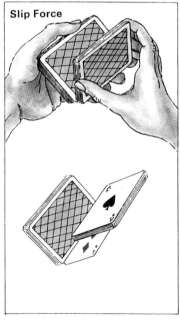

Slip Force

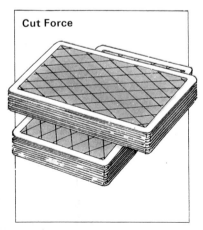

Cut Force

Fan Slip Force

The force card is on the bottom of the pack. FAN the cards out face down. Show the backs to the audience and ask a spectator to point out any card. You cut the pack at the point but at the same time your left fingers push the bottom card into the right fingers. The fan of cards will hide this move and as you cut the pack the force card becomes the bottom card of the right-hand pack of cards. Show the spectator the face of the bottom card (the force card) and say: 'Please remember the card you selected.' You have allowed an apparently free choice, but, in fact, have forced the selection of a particular card.

One-way Force Deck

There are several trick packs which will force a particular card but the simplest, and in many ways the most effective, is the one-way forcing pack. It consists of 52 cards, all of which are identical. Thus, no matter which card the spectator selects, it will be the one you want him to have! As it is rather expensive to make because you will have to buy 52 packs to get 52 cards that are all the same, it is a good idea to buy a one-way force pack from a magical dealer (see page 183).

Two important points to remember when using such a pack are:

1. Never show the faces of the cards or the audience will see that they are all the same.

2. Handle the cards naturally – give them a shuffle before you ask somebody to pick one.

Fan Slip Force

One-way Force Deck

137

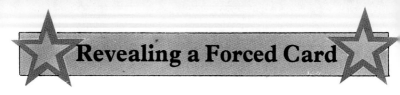

On these pages are two suggestions for revealing a forced card. They turn a simple routine into a complete performance especially if you invent a suitable PATTER to go with each one.

Tearing Tissue

Show a sheet of white tissue paper and a sheet of red, or black, according to the suit of the force card. You then tear them into little pieces and, using a bit of magic, restore them, but they have formed themselves into a replica of the selected card. How do you do it? You will find out by looking back to page 117.

Puppet Prestidigitator

Equipment: A glove puppet, a cardboard box containing a duplicate of the force card, a pack of playing cards.

Performance: Have a card selected (forced) and returned to the pack. Shuffle the pack and then place it in the box – as far away as possible from the duplicate card (so that they don't get mixed up later on).

Now introduce your puppet friend saying that he is a renowned conjurer who will find the selected card. The puppet then goes into the box and starts throwing the cards out one at a time. These are all the wrong cards, so scold the puppet for being so slow. The puppet dives

into the box and throws out a few more cards – this should get the audience laughing. Tell it off again and threaten to ask the spectator to name the chosen card. Immediately get the puppet to pick out the correct card (the duplicate) from the box. Have him bow as the audience applauds.

This method can be very effective if you invent a character for your puppet and develop your patter about its magical abilities. You could give the puppet a blindfold, for example, and tell the audience that you are making the trick more difficult for him because he is such an expert. The puppet then appears to make a mess out of the cards only to produce the right card in the end.

CONJURER'S CHOICE

This is a way to FORCE any one of a number of objects by a process of elimination.

Let us assume there are three objects A, B and C and that you wish to force C. Ask someone to touch two objects. If the spectator touches A and B, then simply remove them and regard C as having been 'chosen'. If A and C are touched, remove B as

it has been eliminated. If B and C are touched, remove A.

Now ask for one object to be pushed towards you. If it is C remove the other object as if C has been chosen. If the other object is moved, simply take it away leaving C.

In this way, whatever the spectator does, C is always the object 'freely selected'.

False Shuffles

It is useful to know how to shuffle a pack of cards in such a way that the position of certain cards, or perhaps of the whole pack, is not disturbed. Here are a few false shuffles you can try. Each must be practised regularly until you can do them, without thinking, at the speed of a normal shuffle. And, as with most SLEIGHTS, you must not look at your hands while you do it.

Quick Cuts

You can give the impression of shuffling the pack, but in fact keeping every card in the same position, as follows. Hold the pack in the right hand in the normal position for shuffling. Drop about half the cards from the top of the pack into the left hand. Then drop all of the remaining cards on top. Pick up the whole pack from the left hand and repeat these moves as often and as fast as you can. With practice it looks as if you are really shuffling the cards. All you are really doing is cutting the pack repeatedly. And, as every magician should know, cutting a pack of cards does not change the order of the cards. This shuffle is useful when you have the whole pack in order, such as in the Eight Kings set-up described on page 132.

Bottom Drop

This method of shuffling but retaining all the cards in sequence requires a little more practice than the last. Hold the pack in the normal shuffling position in the right hand. Bring the two hands together several times as in a normal shuffle. Instead of dropping the cards from the right hand into the left from the top of the pack, however, drop them from the bottom of the right hand pack. Keep doing this until all the cards are in the

Quick cuts

left hand. Once again it looks as if you have shuffled the pack but the cards are still in the same order.

Retaining Top Stock

To keep a batch of cards in position try this. Put the thirteen cards of one suit together at the top of the pack (1). Now begin to shuffle the cards

Bottom drop

140

but on the first drop of cards make sure that you put at least thirteen cards onto the left hand. Shuffle the rest of the cards on top of the first batch but slightly to one side. When you have finished shuffling there should be a definite step in the pack (2). Cut the pack at this point and place the cards from the bottom, the original thirteen cards or more, on to the top. It looks as if the cards were fairly shuffled and then cut but if you now deal out the first thirteen cards they will all be of the one suit.

This shuffle is particularly useful if you wish to do a trick requiring the top few cards of the pack to be in a particular order.

Retaining top stock

Retaining Top Card

This method keeps one card in position on the top of the pack. Hold the pack in your right hand in the normal position for an ordinary overhand shuffle. With the left thumb pull the top card off the pack and into the left hand (1). Now shuffle the rest of the cards on top of the first card in the normal way (2). When the shuffle is finished do it again but this time shuffle normally until you reach the end of the pack (3). Towards the end run the cards singly from the right hand into the left so that what was the bottom card is now replaced on the top (4) – which is where it was originally.

It appears that you have given the pack a straightforward shuffle but the original top card has been retained on the top.

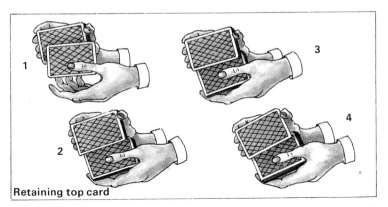

Retaining top card

Your Card

A number of card tricks require the magician to locate a card that has been selected by a spectator and then returned to the pack. There are many ways this trick can be done. This is one of the simplest.

Spread a shuffled pack of cards face down to allow the spectator to remove any card. Ask the spectator to look at his card and remember it. Now ask him to show it to everyone else. This serves two important purposes:

1. It makes certain that the value of the card is remembered.

2. While the attention of the spectators is away from your hands you secretly look at and remember the bottom card.

Now ask the spectator to place his card face down on the top of the pack. Casually cut the pack and complete the cut so the spectator's card is lost in the centre. In fact it is immediately below the card you secretly noted. Cut the pack a few times more so the chosen card seems completely lost. In fact the cutting of the cards will not separate the selected card and your noted card.

To find the spectator's selected card all you have to do is spread the cards in front of you. The card to the right of the card you noted is the selected card.

Noted card

Selected card

PERFORMING YOUR CARD

When performing Your Card it is a good idea to allow a spectator to shuffle the cards first. This proves (without actually mentioning the fact) that the cards are not in any special order. A magician, however, will always make full use of every opportunity that arises. Some people, when they have shuffled the cards, will accidentally allow you to see the face of the bottom card. Secretly make a mental note of this card and carry on with the trick – the only difference being that you do not have to sight the bottom card.

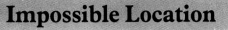

This trick takes some practice but it is well worth the effort for it requires no preparation. Ask a spectator to shuffle a pack of cards and then hand the pack back to you.

Crimp corner

Break

Fan the cards face down and ask someone to take any card, look at it, and remember it. The spectator now pushes the card back anywhere in the pack. Hold the cards tightly as he does this and the card will not go right into the pack. While he is still pushing, you remove the pack from his reach with a slight twisting action. This will cause the selected card to project from the side of the pack.

It is now quite a simple matter to bring up the forefinger of the hand holding the pack and bend down (crimp) the corner of the projecting card. If you practise this so it only takes a moment, no one will be aware that you have done anything crafty.

REMEMBER, REMEMBER

When performing tricks like this one, it is a good idea to ask the spectator to show the card to the rest of the audience. This avoids the trick falling flat if the spectator forgets the card selected and adds extra interest to your presentation.

Immediately the other hand comes over the pack and pushes the selected card flush with the rest of the cards. The pack is then shuffled. It can even be shuffled by a spectator but you can always find the chosen card. All you have to do is look for the BREAK. Just by cutting the cards at that point you can instantly locate the selected card.

With practice you should be break. Just by cutting the cards with the pack held behind your back. As you remove the card from the pack run your fingers over the corner and straighten out the crimp so there will be no clue as to how you accomplished this amazing feat.

The Fabulous Four Aces

1

2

The Four Aces is one of the classics of magic. At the start of your performance go through a pack of cards and remove the aces. Drop each one face up on the table as you find it (1).

Turn the pack face down and hold it in the left hand in the dealing position. Look at one of the spectators and ask: 'Which of these four aces is your favourite?' As you say this the spectators will look at your face, the aces, or at the spectator to whom you are talking. This will enable you secretly to spread the top three cards of the pack slightly to the right, insert your left little finger under the third card and then square up the pack (2).

Pick up the spectator's favourite ace which we will assume to be the Ace of Spades, and place it face up on the top of the pack. Place the other three aces, also face up, on top of the favourite ace.

3

Lift off the top seven cards (four face-up aces and three face-down cards). The break in the pack caused by the little finger makes this move easy to do.

With the left thumb pull the top ace to the left. Name it, then use the remaining cards in the right hand to flip the ace face down on to the pack (3). Do the same with the next two aces. In your right hand you now have the Ace of Spades and, hidden under it, three face-down cards.

144

4

Drop all the cards (handling them as if they are one) from your right hand on top of the pack in your left. Pick up the Ace of Spades and turn it face down on the top of the pack as you say: 'And your favourite ace, the Ace of Spades.' The audience thinks the four aces are on top of the pack – but three indifferent cards are now between the Ace of Spades and the other three aces.

Deal the top four cards (supposedly the aces) face down on to the table (4). Lay them down individually, not in one pile. Then put three cards down on top of each 'ace', making sure the first three cards (the aces) go on top of the Ace of Spades (5).

You now get a spectator to choose one of the four piles. Allow him to think he has a free choice but actually force him to pick the pile that contains the four aces by using the method Conjurer's Choice on page 139.

6

Pick up each of the other piles in turn and reveal each of the three indifferent cards. On the fourth card (which the spectators believe to be an ace) pause dramatically before turning it over to show it has changed from an ace to an indifferent card. It appears that the aces have disappeared. Point to the 'chosen' pile which remains face down on the table. Turn the cards from that pile over one by one – they are the four aces (6).

145

For My Next Trick...

All of the tricks in this section are for performance on a stage or in conditions where the magician has freedom of movement and is at least two metres (six feet) from the audience. Most of the effects can be regarded as classics. Several of them were first performed in the last century and these tricks remain as baffling today as they ever were.

Burnt and Restored Note is a really entertaining and humorous effect in the hands of Terry Seabrooke. This British magician has performed a version of this trick in theatres all over the world and on television in many countries. This trick, together with Cards Across and Silk Through Rope, is particularly useful for the performer who likes to travel light as it needs little in the way of PROPS.

The Afghan Bands was often featured by Harry Blackstone. Although one of America's greatest illusionists, he performed apparent miracles with many smaller effects. The Afghan Bands, Tale of a Donkey's Tail and The Magic Book are especially good tricks to perform for children.

Twentieth Century Silks was a favourite trick of Ade Duval who performed his 'Rhapsody in Silk' in many parts of the USA during the 1920s. His immaculate and colourful magic with SILKS was also greatly admired by audiences in Britain and Europe. Twentieth Century Silks, Soft Soap and Time to Say Goodbye will prove entertaining to most audiences – including children. Something, in fact, for everyone!

◄ **The Chinese Linking Rings,** here performed by Marco the Magi in Le Grand David Show, is a classic magic trick. The rings are first shown to be solid and separate and are then magically linked and unlinked.

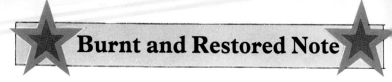

Burnt and Restored Note

Equipment: A banknote, an envelope, four or five boxes that fit inside each other, a pencil, scissors or penknife, a table, an ashtray, matches.

Preparation: Cut a slit about 4 cm (1½ in) long on the face of an envelope. The position of this slit must be where it cannot be seen from the back of the envelope when the envelope is open. Write the number of the banknote lightly in pencil on the inside of the envelope. Place the note in the smallest of the boxes and nest all the boxes together.

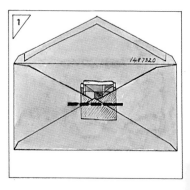

Performance: Ask for the loan of a banknote (the value of which, of course, must be the same as the one concealed in the nested boxes). Take the note and fold it in half, then in half again. Make a third fold in the opposite direction to the other two.

Place the note inside the envelope, keeping the slit concealed behind your hand. Suddenly you realize that no one has made a note of the number. Remove the note from the envelope, unfold it, and pretend to read off the number. Ask someone to write it down or memorize it. What you actually do is read the number from the envelope. Do this boldly and your audience will accept this as absolutely genuine.

Refold the note as before and place it back in the envelope. But this time push it halfway through the slit in the back (1). Show the front of the envelope with the

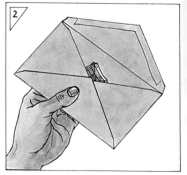

note in position (2). Because the number is written in pencil it will not be seen. But if you are worried about this, cover the number with your thumb when showing the note to the audience.

Seal the envelope. Take the envelope with the right hand, leaving the note concealed in the left (3). The left hand now goes to a pocket for a box of matches and leaves the note in the pocket at the same time.

Set light to one corner of the envelope and, to the dismay of the spectator who loaned you the note, allow it to burn merrily. Drop it into the ashtray on your table so that the envelope can be allowed to burn completely.

You now draw attention to the box on your table. It is handed to the horrified spectator whose note you used. Inside the box is another box. Inside that box is

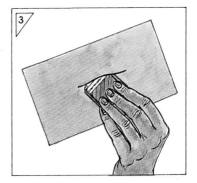

yet another box. And so on ... and so on. When the spectator reaches the last box he finds 'his' banknote and the number is then checked to 'prove' that only one note was used.

ADD SOME HUMOUR

The Burnt and Restored Note can be improved by injecting a little humour into it. One way to do this is to set light to the envelope apparently by accident. You do this by saying that the match is to allow the spectator to see the shadow of his note to prove that it is still in the envelope. Prepare for this by gluing a square of black paper inside the envelope to make the 'shadow'.

After 'proving' that the note is there you continue talking to the audience, forgetting that the match is still alight. The flame touches the envelope 'accidentally' to the horror of the note's owner and the amusement of the audience.

When the envelope is reduced to ashes offer the ashtray to the spectator with apologies for the trick going wrong and you will get another laugh. The opening of the numerous nested boxes will also help to add humour to this excellent trick.

Cards Across

Equipment: Playing cards.

Ask two spectators to assist you. Stand one on your right side and the other on your left, both facing the audience. Remove a pack of cards from its case and while talking to your assistants casually spread the top three cards and insert the tip of your left little finger under the third card.

Palming
a card

Turn to the spectator on your left and hand him the pack. Just before you do this, you place the right hand on top of the pack and secretly take off the top three cards. This is not difficult to do as the little finger helps to push the cards up into your hand.

Keep the three cards concealed in your right hand (this is known as PALMING) as your left hand offers the pack to the spectator – see above right.

Hold your left hand palm up and ask the spectator to count, loud and clear, fifteen cards on to that hand. As soon as the fifteenth card is counted, turn to the spectator on your right and say something like: 'I'll be with you in a minute.' As you turn, bring both hands together and drop the palmed cards from the right hand on to those in the left.

Turn back to the first spectator and ask him to put the 'fifteen' cards into a pocket.

Take the pack back from the first spectator and hand it to the person on the right with the request that she, too, counts fifteen cards on to your left hand. As soon as the twelfth card is counted put the tip of your little finger on it. The three remaining cards are counted on top but the little finger is now holding a break beneath the three top cards. Palm off the three cards as you ask the second spectator if she has a suitable pocket to house the cards. Hand her the cards (now only twelve) and take back the pack in your left hand.

Bring your hands together, and drop the three cards on to the top of the pack as you take the pack in your right hand and drop it into your own pocket.

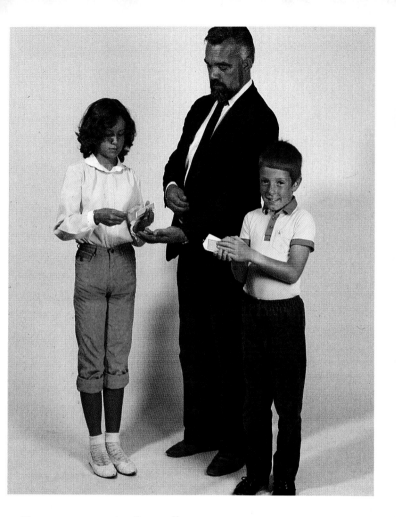

Now announce to the audience that you are going to make three cards travel from one pocket to the other. Pretend to take the cards invisibly one at a time from the second spectator to the first.

Ask the spectator on your right to take the cards from her pocket and to count them on to

▲ **The author** baffling his two assistants in the performance of Cards Across.

your right hand – there are only twelve. Ask the spectator on your left to count his cards on to your left hand – there are eighteen!

151

Twentieth Century Silks

Two SILKS are knotted together and placed somewhere safe. A third silk, of contrasting colour, is vanished and then reappears between the first two silks.

Equipment: Two plain silks, two multicoloured silks, sewing thread, glass tumbler. The two plain silks must be the same colour and at least one corner of the multicoloured silks must be the colour of the plain silks. In this example we will assume that the two plain silks are blue and the multicoloured silks are blue and red.

Preparation: Take one of the blue silks and fold it diagonally in half. Sew the two halves of the silk together from top to bottom about 4 cm (1½ in away from the folded

edge (1). Use sewing thread the same colour as the silk so that the secret preparation will not be visible to the audience.

Tie the blue corner of one multicoloured silk to the top of the prepared blue silk (2). Now push the multicoloured silk into the long secret pocket until just one corner (the corner diagonally opposite the tied corner) is visible. This corner should be a blue one.

Performance: Show two blue silks (one of which is the prepared one) (3) and tie them together (4). In fact you tie one corner of the single blue silk to the exposed corner of the multicoloured silk hidden in the pocket.

Place these 'two' silks into a glass tumbler (5) or stuff them into an

152

assistant's top pocket for safe keeping. Show the duplicate multi-coloured silk to your audience and make it disappear (see box, right).

Grasp one corner of the tied silks and pull it sharply from the tumbler (or pocket). This pulls the multi-coloured silk from the secret pocket and the audience sees the multi-coloured silk tied between the two blue silks (6).

VANISH A SILK

There are hundreds of methods by which a magician can cause a silk to disappear. Here is one you can use for the Twentieth Century Silks. This method can also be used to vanish small objects.

Take two sheets of news-paper and glue them together on three of the four edges so that you end up with a paper bag. Show both sides of the newspaper to your audience and roll it into a cone so that the open unglued edge is at the top. Pretend to place the silk into the cone but really put it in between the two layers of newspaper.

Open out the cone and show the newspaper on both sides once again – the silk has vanished!

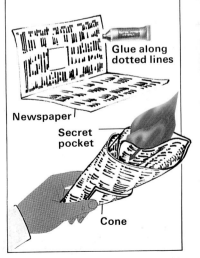

Glue along dotted lines

Newspaper

Secret pocket

Cone

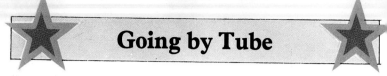

Going by Tube

Equipment: A magazine or large sheet of card, 4 paper clips, 2 pieces of string each about 1.35 m (4½ ft) long.

Roll the magazine or sheet of card into a tube. Use the paper clips to hold it in position. Double the first piece of string and attach the centre of it to the bottom paper clip inside the tube. Pass the second piece of string around the first string and out at the top. When shown to the audience, it will appear that there is a double string running through the tube.

Now pull the strings at the top and the bottom and the tube will move up the strings in a mysterious manner. By pulling on the top strings and relaxing the pull on the lower strings, so that your hands move slightly closer together, the tube will descend. Be careful that you do not allow the linking of the strings to become visible or the audience may work out how the trick is done.

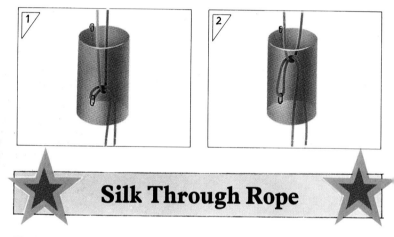

Silk Through Rope

Equipment: A silk and a 2 m (6 ft) length of rope.

In this trick both the silk and the rope are totally unprepared, yet with them you can perform an amazing penetration effect in which the silk appears to pass through the centre of the solid rope.

Ask someone from your audience to hold the rope vertically, one end in each hand. Hold the silk with both hands behind the rope (1). The left

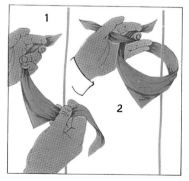

154

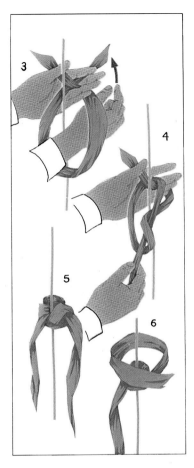

end of the silk should be held between the first and second fingers of the left hand.

Bring the right end of the silk in front of the rope and place it in the left hand (2). Grip part of this right end between the third and fourth fingers of the left hand.

Now put the right hand through the loop you have just formed and pull the original left end of the silk back through the loop (3). Retain the grip of the left-hand third and fourth fingers while doing this so that a small loop is formed as the knot tightens (4).

It looks as if the silk is tied to the rope with a single knot but it is really a slip knot (5). Now bring the right end of the silk around the front of the rope, to the back, and to the right again (6).

Tie the silk in a single knot in front of the rope, making sure that the right end comes back to the right side when the knot is tied, (7) and (8).

Tell the spectator to hold the rope tightly. Pause to obtain the full attention of the audience, then grasp the silk near the knot and pull forward. The silk will come free and it looks as if it has gone right through the rope.

Hold the silk up in both hands. Say, 'There's the rope, there's the handkerchief, there are the knots,' (9), and receive your applause.

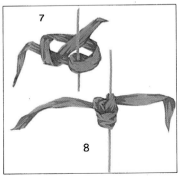

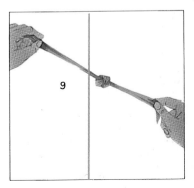

Equipment: Glue, a pair of scissors, three coloured strips of paper, each measuring about 2 m (6 ft) by 7 cm (3 in). The trick is more effective if each strip of paper is a different colour.

Take one strip of the paper and glue the ends together to form a loop (1a and b). Do the same with the second strip but give one end a half turn (turn it over) before joining the ends together (2a and b). With the third strip, give one end a complete turn before gluing the ends (3a and b).

You now have three loops of paper that appear to be exactly the same and quite ordinary. But if you cut them down the centre you will find how different they really are. The first will give you two separate loops (1c) – as you would expect. The second forms two loops – but they are linked together (2c). And the third becomes a single loop (3c), twice the size of the original!

PRESENTING THE AFGHAN BANDS

Invent a Story
Say that, long ago, a magician travelling through Afghanistan was met by a band of fierce tribesmen. They threatened to kill him but the magician saved his life by challenging two of their best swordsmen to slice a coloured ribbon into two separate loops. The magician sliced his ribbon first with no difficulty but the two swordsmen were amazed to find that they produced two linked loops and one very large loop.

Have a Race
Ask for two volunteers from the audience. Give each a band and a pair of scissors. You explain that they are going to have a race and then show them what they will have to do. Take the first band and cut it through the centre to form two separate loops. Emphasize that this is *all* they have to do and say that the first to cut through the centre of his or her loop and produce two separate loops will be the winner. Build up the excitement by encouraging the audience to cheer them on. Of course neither of them wins because they do not end with two separate loops – one has two loops linked together and the other has one loop.

◄ **The Afghan Bands** performed by the author and his two assistants. This is a useful trick to learn as the props are simple but colourful. It makes an effective stage performance if you use the help of two people from the audience. But, if your volunteers are very young, don't race them against each other – they might cut themselves in the excitement.

Equipment: Six large SILKS, an empty soap powder packet, a cardboard tube (a section from a roll of kitchen foil will be fine), clear adhesive tape, string, a button, sewing thread, a blunt knife.

Preparation: Dirty three of the large silks with earth, indian ink, tomato ketchup – anything you like. Fold one of the clean silks in half and sew up two sides. Sew a button on to one corner and draw a string around it so that it hangs down on two sides within the sewn-up handkerchief. Attach the cardboard tube to the string with tape (1).

Open the empty soap powder packet very carefully, using a blunt knife to open the top, bottom and sides at the glued sections without cutting the cardboard. Open the packet out flat and brush off any soap powder that may be sticking to it. Reassemble the box and use a small piece of adhesive tape to hold the bottom and sides closed.

Put the FAKED (prepared) silk in the box with the open end uppermost. Alongside this place the two other clean silks (2).

Performance: Show the three dirty silks. Then put them, one at a time, into the soap powder

158

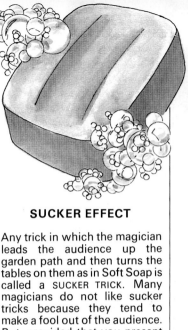

packet. As you do this, secretly push them into the hidden tube.

Close the box and then shake it around to imitate the action of a washing machine. As part of this MOVE turn the box over. Open the box by unsticking the adhesive tape, take out the first clean silk and place it on the table.

By this time some people will be pointing out that you turned the box over. Appear to ignore these remarks and remove the second clean silk. This is actually the faked silk but if you hold it by the button the tube will hang down within the folds of the silk and its presence will not be

suspected. Place this silk on the table, preferably behind something or into a container of some kind. Remove the final silk with a flourish and take a bow.

By now your audience will be complaining loudly that you cheated by turning the box over. Look inside the box and say: 'But the box is empty.'

This will probably bring demands that you prove your claim. Try to wriggle out of this but eventually give in to the demands and open the box out flat. Much to the audience's surprise, there is absolutely nothing in it!

159

Time to say Goodbye

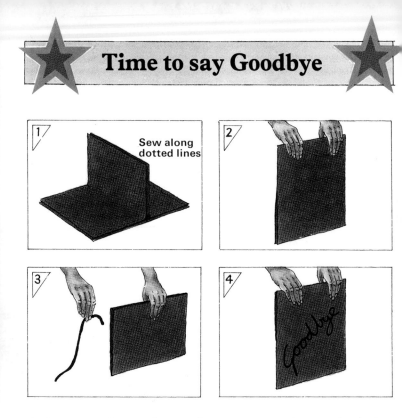

Sew along dotted lines

Equipment: Three pieces of material all the same size, (about 30 cm (12 in) by 40 cm (16 in), and colour, two pieces of ribbon about 1 m (3 ft) long, sewing thread, chalk.

Preparation: Place one piece of material on the table and lay a second piece on top of it. Sew the two pieces together along the top edge and *exactly* halfway down each side.

Now fold the bottom edge of the uppermost piece up to the top edge and place the third piece of material on top. Sew the two bottom edges together and half-

way up the sides as before. Then sew the second and third pieces along the edges. You now have a banner with a movable flap which can be placed to cover either the top or the bottom of the banner (1).

Place the flap so that it lies flush with the top edge and, with a piece of chalk, write the word 'Goodbye' in one continuous line. Sew one of the pieces of ribbon over the chalk to form the word as shown in (4).

Performance: Hold the banner with the flap hanging down-wards so that the banner appears blank (2). Fold the bottom (both edges) up to form a double bag (3). Then show the second piece of ribbon and drop it into the rear part of the bag. Drop the front thickness of material and it appears that the loose ribbon has magically become the word 'Goodbye' (4). In fact the ribbon that you showed to the audience remains hidden in the top half of the banner. Practise the trick so that the audience cannot detect the slight movement of your fingers as you alter your grip on the folds of material.

The Tale of a Donkey's Tail

This interesting and unusual trick makes use of the Goodbye banner principle.

Equipment: Draw or embroider the outline of a donkey or a dog minus its tail on each side of the banner. On one of the drawings attach a length of ribbon to the hindquarters of the donkey or dog to represent its tail.

Performance: The animal is first shown without its tail (1). Then the banner is formed into a bag, and the ribbon is dropped into the rear part of the bag as in 'Time to Say Goodbye'. When the banner is opened (2), there is the tail in the proper place!

1

2

If you like, you can tell the audience a story about the donkey losing its tail and how a great magician (you of course!) managed to find it and put it back where it belonged.

The Magic Book

With this magic book a number of effects are possible. You can, for example, flick through the book and show that it contains blank pages only. Yet when it is flicked through a second time you reveal that it is full of stamps. Or, you can make it a painting book – on the first flick through the pictures are outlines only but when you flick through again every picture is beautifully painted. When you have read how to make the book, see if you can think of some other ideas.

Equipment: A scrapbook or exercise book, scissors, stamps, coloured pencils or paints.
Preparation: Making the magic book will probably take some time but it is not difficult. Cut about 5 mm

($\frac{1}{4}$ in) off the top righthand corner of the first page and every alternate page from then on. Next cut the same amount off the bottom right-hand corner of the second page and every alternate page. The pages with the top corner cut are the ones on which you stick the stamps or paint pictures.

Decorate the cover of the book according to the type of presentation you intend to use. For example, if you are going to use it as a painting effect you could draw a large paint brush and palette on the cover with the words *Magic Painting Book*.

To show the book with blank pages flick through it from the front to the back with your thumb at the top corner. To make the paintings or stamps appear you put your thumb at the bottom righthand corner.

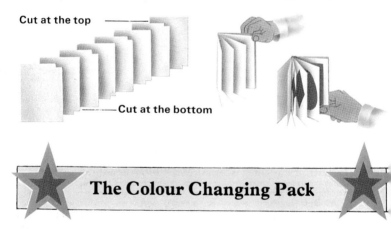

Cut at the top

Cut at the bottom

The Colour Changing Pack

Equipment: Two packs of playing cards (one red-backed, one blue-backed).
The principle used for The Magic Book can also be applied to playing cards. Take 26 cards from each pack – trim the right-hand corner of

162

the red-backed cards and the left corner of the blue-backed cards – and put them together alternating red and blue throughout the 52 cards. By riffling the cards at one corner, you can show the cards as all blue. If you riffle at the opposite corner, the pack appears to be red.

Actual cut size

Alternate red and blue cards

★ An Amazing Prediction ★

Here is a good trick that you can do with the Colour Changing Pack above. Show the cards as all blue. Riffle through them again (with your thumb on the right corner) with the faces towards the audience and ask a spectator to stop you at any point. When you stop he is to take the card facing him (this will be a red-backed card). Place it, face up, on the table.

Say: 'Earlier today I placed a red-backed card in this pack. (Riffle the cards showing them as blue.) Will you please tell me the name of the card you selected.' When the spectator answers, say, 'Believe it or not that is the very card that I thought you would select from this blue-backed pack of cards.'

The spectator turns his card over. It is seen to have a red back!

On With The Show

David Devant, one of the greatest magicians of all time, said that: 'To say that a man who can show a few tricks is a magician is as absurd as to say that a man who can recite *The Merchant of Venice* by heart is an actor'. He meant that just to be able to do a trick is not enough. Certainly you should practise your tricks until you can do them well. But you must also think about the way you present your effects to make them entertaining to the audience.

Magicians have always been first and foremost entertainers. Some of the most amazing tricks have quite simple solutions as you will have seen if you have read the descriptions of the tricks carefully. It is how you present them – not what you *do* but what the audience *thinks* you do – that turns them into magic.

One of the world's most famous conjurers, Harry Houdini, was possibly the greatest showman ever. From 1900 to his death in 1926 he amazed spectators with his sensational stunts and fantastic escapes. He managed to get out of the toughest jails, the safest of safes and the strongest handcuffs and manacles that could be forged. He once escaped from a giant laced-up football and on at least one occasion he got out of a huge, sealed paper bag without tearing it. This king of escapology used similar principles to escape each time but he also varied the presentation of his tricks. Because each performance was different from the last and seemingly more impossible he was able to divert his audience from the methods used.

In this chapter we will concentrate on the basic rules of magic and how to put an entertaining act together. Remember that these rules are just as important as the methods by which the tricks are accomplished. If you practise these thoroughly you will be able to present an interesting and entertaining act of professional quality.

The Importance of Practice

Even though you may have no desire to be a professional magician you should always strive to achieve a professional performance. Your act should be as perfect as you can make it. To reach this perfection it is essential that you practise every aspect of your performance as completely as possible. Continual practice will give you absolute

▶ **Magic is always** popular with children and the magician's rabbit is an instant success in this magic show.

◀ **A mirror** allows you to see your performance as the audience sees it. It will also enable you to make sure you are carrying out each move correctly.

▶ **Sorcar** sawing one of his women assistants in half with a buzz-saw. This trick caused a sensation when it was performed on television in 1956. At the finish the camera cut to another performer and viewers assumed that the girl had died.

confidence in your ability to do the trick correctly. You can then forget about the mechanics of the effect and pay full attention to the presentation of the trick and to your most important function as a magician – entertaining the audience.

Practising a trick should be an active, not passive, activity. This means that you must think while you are practising. Do not be a practising parrot – think about what you are doing. In what way can the trick be improved? What are the weak points of the trick and how can they be concealed, strengthened or eliminated? Is the action logical? Are the moves natural? Would it be better if a certain remark or action was left out? Is that the way you would normally do a MOVE if you were actually performing magic? These are some of the questions you should be asking – and answering – during your practice sessions.

Practising with a Mirror

It is a good idea to practise new tricks in front of a mirror. This will help you to make sure that you are carrying out the various moves correctly. Even when you are confident that you have got the routine right you will find it useful to work through the trick in front of a mirror occasionally to detect any faults in your performance.

A mirror is also extremely useful when you are practising a trick in which the angle of observation is critical. This is particularly true of

166

certain SLEIGHTS which can be seen effectively only when viewed from one point. The mirror will teach you where to position yourself in relation to your audience. It will warn you, too, of the places from which the weak points in the trick may be glimpsed.

Using a mirror in practice will also help you to lose the habit of looking at your hands in performance. Spectators tend to look wherever the magician looks and it is often necessary to stop them looking at your hands. A mirror will train you to look elsewhere while your hands are carrying out a trick.

Four Golden Rules

Whether you wish to perform magic as an amateur or as a professional it is important that you follow the four golden rules of successful conjuring. These rules apply just as much to simple or easy tricks as they do to more complicated effects. They are:

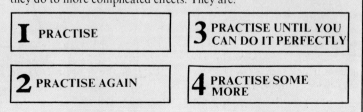

1 PRACTISE	**3** PRACTISE UNTIL YOU CAN DO IT PERFECTLY
2 PRACTISE AGAIN	**4** PRACTISE SOME MORE

The Magician's Image

As a magician your appearance – style of dress and manner of behaviour – is a crucial part of your performance. It is one of the most important ways in which you establish yourself as a real magician in the minds of your spectators.

Before the 1800s, most conjurers wore long all-concealing robes and tall wizard-like hats. But since then magicians have been far more varied in their style. Some present themselves as exotic figures. In the early 1900s, for example, William Ellsworth Robinson performed as Chung Ling Soo, the 'Celestial Chinese Conjurer'. His spectacular show

included the Bullet Catching Trick in which he caught the bullets fired by two assistants dressed as Chinese warriors. Chung Ling Soo's impersonation was kept up throughout his act and even off-stage. He wore Chinese make-up, spoke in 'Chinese' that was interpreted for his audience, wore Chinese costume and had Chinese stories to cover all his tricks. Few other magicians have gone to such lengths in their presentation.

Today most magicians just dress smartly in a suit or in more casual clothes.

Choosing Your Image

Whether you decide to appear in exotic dress or just in your usual clothes is up to you. But as a magician you must at all times look smart. Your clothes must be clean and neatly pressed. Your shoes should be highly polished and your hair, hands and nails should be perfectly groomed. This means that you must not bite your nails, for in close-up magic especially, the hands are the centre of attention.

The question of appearance also extends to your properties or PROPS – the objects used in your performance. They must be clean, freshly polished or painted. It should never be obvious to the audience that they are simply bits of cardboard joined together with sticky tape or bits of string even if they are. Always keep these two points in mind:

1. The apparatus should be in keeping with the presentation of the trick. For example, if you are doing an act dressed up as a Chinese Magician, then your props should look Chinese. If you use the Square Circle Production it should be decorated to look like a pagoda, the Torn and Restored paper should have Chinese characters written on it, and so on. If, however, you are doing a straightforward conjuring act your apparatus should not look unusual unless you explain it away in your patter by saying something like: 'This strange device is the latest scientific invention.' In fact, there is an idea for a complete act: Wear a white coat and spectacles and make all your props look like scientific apparatus. You can then do your act in the manner of a scientist giving a lecture.

2. All apparatus and the properties used should be kept in immaculate condition. If you are asked to do a show, make sure everything is clean, the silks are not creased and your appearance is as perfect as can be.

When you are thinking about your image, remember that it is very important to show your tricks in a way that suits your personality. If you are naturally cheerful and talkative then jokes in your act will not seem out of place. You will also be able to tell them without losing your concentration. If you are more

▲ **Chung Ling Soo** (William Ellsworth Robinson) often performed the effect of shooting a ribbon through a girl assistant.

serious-minded then it may be better to present your tricks as scientific experiments. Most people have a personality somewhere between these two extremes and will find that a casual and friendly style of presentation is most effective.

Look and Learn
One of the best ways to go about choosing and developing your presentation is to watch other

169

▲ **The magician** Ali Bongo in his colourful costume as 'The Shriek of Araby'. He is magical adviser to many television shows, including *The Paul Daniels Show*.

performers. But do not just watch magicians. Watch all performers of entertainment – and entertainment of all kinds. If you wish, for example, to present a silent act to music, watch professional ice skaters to see how their movements blend in with the music. Try to achieve the same synchronization in your act. If you wish to present an act with a comic patter, watch the great comedians and see how they time their jokes. And, of course, watch the good magicians. They

may present the same tricks as you but look how their audiences are transfixed. Watch them carefully to see how they present their effects and you will pick up useful hints on how to get and hold the interest of your spectators and produce 'real' magic.

Make an Entrance
Your entrance on stage is a most important part of your act. The impact your appearance makes as you walk on sets the tone for the rest of the performance. If you are presenting a smart modern act, your entry should be brisk and confident. If you are performing in the character of a lazy magician, then amble casually on to the stage. In the same

way make sure you perform each trick in a way that fits in with the image you have chosen.

Smile

During your performance make a point of looking at every part of the audience. This should not be done automatically but with a genuine desire to include all the spectators in your act. You must regard each spectator as a personal friend and treat them all as such. Contact between performer and spectator is essential as every successful entertainer knows. If you look at what you are doing, at the ceiling or at the back of the hall then you will not make this contact and may even lose your audience's interest altogether.

Learning how to smile is an important part of the technique of making contact with your audience. You may be nervous and you may be wondering if a trick will work or not, but you must not show it. *Smile*. Give the audience the impression that you are enjoying what you are doing and that you welcome their company. If you smile you will get the audience on your side, ready to appreciate and see what *you* want them to see.

Coping With Stage Fright

Many performers – even experienced professionals – suffer with what is known as 'stage fright'. Stage fright usually does not arise from fear but is caused by excitement. It can do you no harm. If you are well rehearsed and completely familiar with every aspect of your act you should have nothing to fear.

Try not to let stage fright worry you. A dozen deep breaths before walking on stage will help calm your nerves and allow your mind to concentrate on entertaining your audience. Once you get into your act you will probably find that the butterflies in your stomach fly away. To help this happen even faster choose a trick you can do well as your first number. Once you are well into your act, the enjoyment in entertaining your audience will help make your nervousness vanish.

The best antidote for stage fright is confidence in your performance. This comes only through continual practice, attention to detail and experience.

Putting an Act Together

A performance of magic is not merely a collection of tricks strung together in a haphazard way. It is a carefully thought out programme in which the individual effects are arranged so that, as far as possible, each item blends smoothly into the next. Each trick should contribute to the building of the complete act so the routine as a whole proceeds to a logical climax.

When deciding upon a programme of your own it is useful to bear certain rules in mind to make sure that your act achieves this logical build-up. Some programmes are given as examples on page 175 but by following these rules you will be able to produce several good magic acts of your own using the tricks from this book.

Pace and Variety

First of all it is a good idea to start the act with either a quick trick or one that immediately establishes in the minds of the audience the fact that you are a magician. The second trick can then be done at a more leisurely pace. The tricks that follow should be more dramatic, each increasing in its effect until the climax is reached.

For the last-but-one effect you should choose a trick that slows the act down slightly. Then move straight into your last trick which should be one that will achieve the maximum impact. As far as possible it should be baffling and spectacular. Most PRODUCTIONS and ILLUSIONS fall into this category.

Secondly, while choosing and practising the presentation of tricks remember these two important words: pace and variety. Some tricks should be performed slowly and deliberately, others should be fast and dramatic. Make sure that your programme

▼ **The finale** of the Square Circle Production. The production box can be decorated in a number of ways so that you can weave an entertaining story around the trick (see page 45).

contains tricks of both kinds. To achieve variety in your act do tricks that are completely different in their effect from the ones before and after. Never, for example, do the Cut and Restored Rope and the Torn and Restored paper in the same act or the Organ Pipes and the Square Circle Production. Although these tricks may be different to you because they use different methods, they appear the same to the audience if they are performed within a few minutes of each other.

Lastly, select tricks to suit as far as possible your audience and the occasion. Bear in mind that some tricks are more appreciated by certain groups of people than others and be adaptable. For example, if you are performing Time to Say Goodbye in a particular place, the word that 'writes' itself on the banner could be the name of the town. If you are taking part in a Christmas show, produce Santa Claus in Production Extraordinaire.

▼ **A magician** and his back-stage assistants arrange props on the stage before the start of a performance. The correct positioning of everything helps to make the show run smoothly.

A Family Show

Putting on a family show can be great fun. But you will still have to plan your act carefully to suit the mixed ages of your spectators and especially to hold the attention of very young children. Keep your magic colourful, full of action and entertaining. Do not choose any complicated tricks that require your audience to concentrate for long periods of time.

It is a good idea to involve your spectators wherever possible. Use assistants from the audience whenever you can – even if it is only to hold something used in the trick. Get your audience to clap your helpers at the end of an effect. Ask them to shout out any magic words you use – and make these words funny. If you appear to be losing your audience's attention, try slotting in one of the comedy items described on pages 178–179 or a continuity gag like Clippo (see page 35). Think up other jokes that you could include.

▼ **A magician** being helped by a spectator at a children's party. It is important to involve members of the audience in the tricks wherever possible, especially when performing for children.

174

Conjuring for children is a very popular branch of magic among professional magicians. Practise your presentation by putting on as many shows you can for your friends and family and you will soon find out the rewards of amazing them all.

New Tricks

Where do new tricks come from? The answer is that they are invented by magicians who take the trouble to think about their magic. This means that they examine every new idea that they come across and try to see how it can be used in magic. They also spend a great deal of time thinking about the tricks they perform and how they can be improved.

Look at the tricks you do and see if there is any way you can develop them – perhaps for a special show. Try altering tricks by doing them with different equipment. Most card tricks, for example, look completely different if they are done with picture postcards. Similarly, try performing coin tricks with buttons or with sweets for a children's party. By decorating your props in special ways or by using different objects, one trick can be turned into two.

Ask yourself what the effect would be if you performed it in reverse order or if you combined two tricks together. With thought, many of the tricks in this book can be adapted and made into new tricks. Look at them carefully – you may be surprised at the results you achieve.

The Rules of Magic

As we have seen, the way you present your tricks is extremely important – much more so than what you actually do. The simplest of tricks, presented by a good magician, can appear both baffling and entertaining. And learning how to be entertaining is one of the most important tasks for any magician.

If you follow the suggestions in this chapter you will be ready to present your first magic show. Try putting on a number of performances in front of audiences of different ages and types. You will find that this varied experience will give you plenty of ideas on how to improve your show as well as the confidence and smoothness you need in performance.

When you have given a great number of performances you will come to know instinctively what is good or bad in your act. But until then think about the information in this chapter and keep to the following basic rules:

1. Never tell anyone how the tricks are done. The basic appeal of magic is that the audience does not know how your miracles are accomplished. As soon as you tell someone the secret you destroy the illusion that you are a great magician.

2. Never repeat a trick. If you do the same trick in quick succession people will have a better chance of working out how it is done the second time.

3. Always practise your tricks in private before showing them to anyone. If you are not absolutely certain of what you are doing you will give a bad performance with no magic about it.

4. Be neat and tidy. Keep your apparatus clean and smart. If you are scruffy and untidy and your equipment tatty, your performance is likely to be slipshod and your audience will soon lose interest.

5. Try not to worry about stage fright. Even professional magicians are nervous before they do a show. The best way to avoid unnecessary worry is to practise your act until you know that you can do it perfectly. You will then be able to concentrate on giving a good show without the strain of wondering whether any of your tricks may not have come off properly.

6. Read all you can about magic and magicians. If there is a magic society you can join, then join it. If not, why not form your own? By thinking about and talking about magic you will develop new ideas and possibly invent tricks that no one else knows.

176

7. Make your performance entertaining. Watch other magicians and you will see that they do not just demonstrate the tricks mechanically. They make jokes, they tell stories, they sometimes use music to enhance their act. Perhaps you could do the same. Learn by watching other magicians but do not copy their acts. The best magicians add their own original touches to the tricks that they perform.

8. Believe that you are a real magician. This may sound funny advice, but if you do not believe that you are a real magician, how can you expect your audience to do so? As David Devant said, a good magician is an actor playing the part of a magician. To be a good magician you must be a good actor and believe in what you are doing.

▶ **The clubroom** of the world famous Magic Circle in London where members meet for shows, lectures and other events. It has its own private theatre, two libraries and a museum.

▼ **The Magic Castle,** a popular magic club in Hollywood, USA, where magicians from all over the world meet to discuss their art and to present magic.

Comedy Props

As a general rule spectators like their magic to be funny and entertaining. Here are a few comedy PROPS you can make which will inject some laughs into your act.

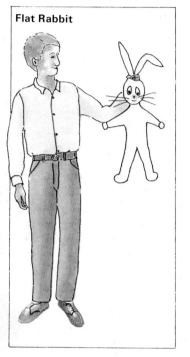

Flat Rabbit

Chicken Sandwich

Flat Rabbit

Announce that you often produce a rabbit during your act. Unfortunately, you cannot show the trick today as you have just had your clothes pressed. As you say this you reach into an inside pocket and remove a flattened rabbit. This is simply a rabbit cut from a piece of felt with two small pieces of felt used to form the eyes.

Chicken Sandwich

Cut the shape of a scrawny chicken from a piece of white felt. Attach two small pieces of red felt for the chicken's comb. Paint two pieces of wood so that they look like bread. Glue the chicken's head to one slice and the feet to the other. Fold the chicken between the two slices. During your act pick up the sandwich from the table. Tell

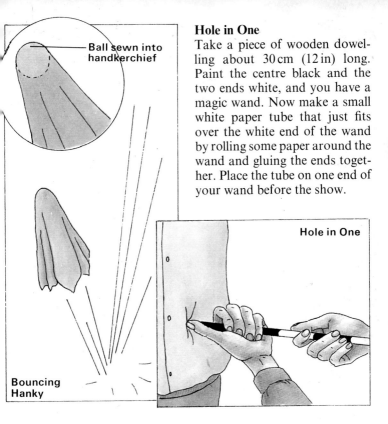

Ball sewn into handkerchief

Bouncing Hanky

Hole in One

Take a piece of wooden dowelling about 30 cm (12 in) long. Paint the centre black and the two ends white, and you have a magic wand. Now make a small white paper tube that just fits over the white end of the wand by rolling some paper around the wand and gluing the ends together. Place the tube on one end of your wand before the show.

Hole in One

your audience that it is a chicken sandwich and let the bottom slice fall to reveal the chicken.

Bouncing Hanky

During your act take out your handkerchief to mop your brow. You then deliberately throw the handkerchief on to the floor. Much to the surprise of everyone in the audience the handkerchief bounces right back into your hand. A small rubber ball cleverly sewn into the centre of the handkerchief is the secret behind this particular joke.

At any time you can invite a spectator up and appear to bore a hole into his body.

Stand with your right side facing the audience. Place the tip of the wand against the volunteer's body. Cover the tip with your left hand and push the shell along the wand towards him. If you keep the end of the wand nearest you hidden behind your right arm it looks as if you are really boring a hole into him. Pull the shell back along the wand and it looks as if you are pulling the wand out again.

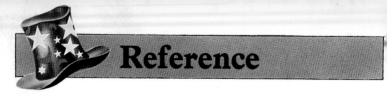

Magic Facts

There are many important dates in the history of magic and thousands of astounding magicians. Unfortunately, this list can include only a few.

BC
c.1700 *Westcar Papyrus* (now in the State Museum, East Berlin) records the earliest known performance of conjuring as an entertainment.

AD
1584 Jean Prévost published the first French book on practical magic, *La Premiere Partie des Subtiles et Plaisantes Inventions* (The First Part of Subtle and Pleasant Tricks).

1584 Publication of *The Discoverie of Witchcraft* by Reginald Scot, the first English book to explain the methods of conjuring.

1734 Jacob Meyer born in Philadelphia, Pennsylvania, USA. Meyer, using the name 'Philadelphia', was the first American magician to win fame in Europe.

1769 Baron Wolfgang von Kempelen, a Hungarian noble, invents 'The Automatic Chess Player'. Although not designed as a magical illusion, it baffled many people and introduced new methods of concealment and misdirection that have been used by illusionists ever since.

1814 Birth of John Henry Anderson, 'The Great Wizard of the North', who performed with 'solid silver' apparatus.

1845 Robert-Houdin, 'the father of modern magic', presents his first Soirée Fantastique in Paris.

1853 Adelaide Herrmann, possibly the world's greatest female magician, is born in London. She took over from her husband, Alexander Herrmann, when he died in 1896.

1856 Robert-Houdin uses his magic to quell a threatened uprising in Algeria.

1873 Maskelyne and Cooke first perform at The Egyptian Hall, England's Home of Mystery, in London.

1874 Ehrich Weiss born in Budapest. As Harry Houdini he performed all over the world.

1905 The Magic Circle formed in London. It is the world's most famous magical society.

1911 The Great Lafayette dies in a fire at the Empire Theatre,

Edinburgh. His body was cremated but then a second body was found and also identified as The Great Lafayette – the first body had been that of a double who featured in some of the illusions.

1926 Harry Houdini dies. The date of his death, October 31, is marked as National Magic Day in the USA.

1936 The British magician Fred Culpitt becomes the first magician to perform on television.

1961 Main Street in Colon, Michigan, USA, is renamed Blackstone Avenue in honour of the illusionist Harry Blackstone.

1963 The Magic Castle in Hollywood, California, USA, is opened.

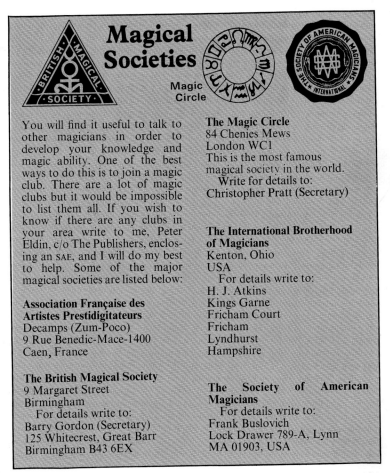

Magical Societies

Magic Circle

You will find it useful to talk to other magicians in order to develop your knowledge and magic ability. One of the best ways to do this is to join a magic club. There are a lot of magic clubs but it would be impossible to list them all. If you wish to know if there are any clubs in your area write to me, Peter Eldin, c/o The Publishers, enclosing an SAE, and I will do my best to help. Some of the major magical societies are listed below:

Association Française des Artistes Prestidigitateurs
Decamps (Zum-Poco)
9 Rue Benedic-Mace-1400
Caen, France

The British Magical Society
9 Margaret Street
Birmingham
   For details write to:
Barry Gordon (Secretary)
125 Whitecrest, Great Barr
Birmingham B43 6EX

The Magic Circle
84 Chenies Mews
London WC1
This is the most famous magical society in the world.
   Write for details to:
Christopher Pratt (Secretary)

The International Brotherhood of Magicians
Kenton, Ohio
USA
   For details write to:
H. J. Atkins
Kings Garne
Fricham Court
Fricham
Lyndhurst
Hampshire

The Society of American Magicians
   For details write to:
Frank Buslovich
Lock Drawer 789-A, Lynn
MA 01903, USA

Magic Book List

The art of conjuring is a vast subject and it is not possible to cover everything in one book. A magician should read as much as possible to develop knowledge of magic and skill. There are, however, so many books on conjuring that selecting which ones to read becomes rather difficult. The books listed on this page are extremely useful. Some of them are very expensive but you might be lucky and find them in your local library. If you want to buy the books and find it difficult to obtain them through a bookshop, try writing to one of the magic dealers listed opposite. They should be able to get you a copy or tell you where you can obtain one. It is always worth looking for magic books in secondhand bookshops. You might well pick up a bargain.

The Big Book of Magic by Patrick Page (Sphere). A wide-ranging book of magical effects – from close-up tricks to large scale illusions.

Card Tricks Without Skill by Paul Clive, (Faber and Faber). Over a hundred card tricks – a must if you want to perform with cards.

The Complete Magician by Marvin Kaye, (Pan Books). Explains how tricks are done and how to perform them – every magician should read this.

The Great Illusionists by Edwin A. Dawes (Chartwell Books). A history of magic.

Modern Magic, More Magic, Later Magic, Three books all by Professor Hoffmann (Routledge). Written over a hundred years ago, the principles outlined in these books remain valid and interesting to the serious magician.

Panorama of Magic and Panorama of Prestidigitators by Milbourne Christopher (Dover Publications). Two illustrated books on the history of magic.

Sucessful Conjuring for Amateurs by Norman Hunter (C. Arthur Pearson Ltd). You won't be able to perform most of the tricks in this book unless you are rich enough to buy the apparatus required. But if you want to know how to levitate a person or make someone vanish, this book will tell you how it's done.

The Tarbell Course in Magic by Harlan Tarbell (Louis Tannen). A complete (but expensive) 7-volume course in magic.

As well as books, magazines that specialize in magic can be very useful. Write for details on the following to the addresses given:

Abracadabra
Goodliffe Productions Ltd.
150 New Road
Bromsgrove, Worcestershire
Magigram
Supreme Magic Co. Ltd
64 High Street
Bideford, Devon
Magic Info
International Magic Studio
89 Clerkenwell Road
London EC1
Genii
Box 36068
Los Angeles
California 90036, USA

Magic Dealers

As well as learning tricks from books such as this one it is also possible to buy tricks from magical dealers. Most of them issue catalogues or lists describing the effects. These lists must be bought from the dealer. Write first asking if he has a catalogue and how much it is (most dealers refund the cost of the catalogue when they receive your first order). When writing make sure you enclose a stamped addressed envelope for the reply.

L. Davenport and Co.
Charing Cross Underground
Shopping Concourse,
The Strand
London WC2N 4HZ

International Magic Studio
89 Clerkenwell Road
London EC1

Kovari Magic Productions
465 Watford Way
London NW4

Magitrix
2b Hope Street, Hanley
Stoke-on-Trent ST1 5PS

Repro 71
48 Emu Road
London SW8

The Supreme Magic Co.
64 High Street
Bideford, Devon

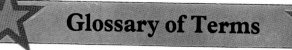

Magic, like all specialist subjects, has its own language and its own technical terms. The ones used in this book are explained here briefly. Wherever possible, explanations refer back to tricks so that you can find out what the word means in practice. Some terms are not used in this book but you may need to know them if you want to talk with other magicians or when you read books on conjuring.

Acquitment The secret transfer of a concealed object from hand to hand to enable both hands to be shown apparently empty.

Angles The magician should always be aware of what the audience can see when he is performing. Some tricks can only be viewed from certain positions. When performing close-up these angles of visibility become specially important. See page 23.

Backpalm A sleight that allows the hand to be shown empty at the time concealing something behind the fingers.

Black Art A principle that states that anything painted black cannot be seen when placed against a black background. See page 45.

Book Test Any mental effect using a book or several books in which the mentalist predicts or divines a word or words selected by a spectator. See page 75.

Close-up Magic Tricks designed to be performed with the magician close to the audience.

Continuity Gag A joke that is repeated several times during an act. A trick that appears to go wrong each time the magician tries it is one type of continuity gag. See page 35.

Double Backed Card A playing card that has no face. Both sides of the card show the back design.

Double Faced Card A card that has no back. Both sides of the card show a face. It could show the same card on each side, or different cards, for example Three of Diamonds on one side and Ten of Hearts on the other.

Double Lift A sleight in which two cards are lifted from the pack but the audience believes that only one card was removed. See pages 130-131.

Effect The trick as it appears to the spectators.

Fake A gimmick. Often spelt feke.

False Count A count of cards or other objects which appears genuine but where the number of objects is more or less than it seems to be. See pages 40-43 and 100-101.

False Cut An apparently fair cut of a pack of cards that does not disturb the order of the pack.

False Shuffle An apparently fair shuffle that keeps all, or some cards, in a set order. See pages 140-141.

Fan Spreading the cards to form a neat fan shape. To make this move easier magicians use fanning powder.

Fanning Powder Powder, usually French chalk, applied to cards to make them slippery and therefore easier to fan.

Finale The finish to a trick or an act – usually something bigger or more impressive than whatever has gone before.

Finger Palm The concealment of an object between the fingers of the hand. See page 106.

Flash Paper A chemically treated paper that creates a brilliant flash when ignited.

Force To give a spectator an apparently free choice but really making him select a predetermined card, colour, number and so on. See pages 136-137 and Conjurer's Choice on page 139.

Foulard A very large scarf or silk.

Gimmick A secret piece of equipment.

Glide A sleight in which the magician retains the bottom card of the pack and deals the next card as if it were the bottom card. See pages 128-129.

Keys or Locators These are specially prepared cards that can be easily located in a pack of cards. See pages 126-127.

Illusion A stage trick using people or large animals. Often illusions involve the vanishing, production or apparent mutilation of people.

Lapping The technique of secretly dropping cards or other objects on the lap while seated at a table. See pages 22-23.

Legerdemain Sleight-of-hand.

Levitation The effect of something or someone floating in the air without visible means of support.

▲ A finger palm.

Load 1. Object or objects to be produced. 2. The introduction of a load into a piece of apparatus. See page 67.

Misdirection The art of drawing the spectator's attention away from a secret move. This is one of the most important aspects of the art of conjuring and is best learnt from experience. See pages 22-23 and 54.

Move The execution of a sleight or other secret movement.

One Ahead A principle of mentalism in which the performer is at least one move ahead of the audience. See pages 77 and 135.

Palm or palming The concealment of an object in the palm of the hand. See pages 150-151 and also **back palm, thumb palm** and **finger palm.**

Patter The storyline, jokes or other talk used by a magician.

Production Making things appear from thin air (see The Miser's Dream on page 66) or from an apparently empty container (see Square Circle Production on page 45).

Props This is short for properties – the apparatus and other objects used by a performer.

Pull A gimmick that vanishes an object by pulling it up the sleeve or beneath the jacket.

Riffle To flick the ends of a pack of cards in order to make a clicking noise or to show the cards.

Routine The order of events that make up a trick or a series of tricks that follow one another in an act.

Servante A concealed shelf at the rear of a chair or table.

Set-up 1. The secret arrangement of playing cards. This can be just a few cards or the whole

▼ **The thumb palm.**

pack depending on the trick to be performed. See pages 132-135.
2. The way props and gimmicks are arranged for a trick.

Silk A square of silk or silk handkerchief.

Sleight A skilful movement of the fingers by which a magical effect is accomplished. See pages 56-57.

Sleight-of-hand The performance of sleights.

Spring goods Items, containing springs, that can be squashed into a small space prior to production. They expand to their normal size when produced.

Steal To secretly remove something from the place where it is concealed.

Sucker Trick A trick in which the magician lets the audience believe that they have worked out how the trick is done or that they have seen the magician make a mistake. Then he proves them wrong at the end. See pages 158-159.

Switch To secretly exchange one thing for another.

Talk The accidental sound made by something hidden, thus revealing its presence to the audience. For example: the clinking of coins in a hand which is supposed to be empty. See page 111.

Thumb Palm The secret concealment of an object by holding it at the base of the thumb and first finger. See pages 106-109.

Well A secret pocket in a magician's table.

Index